SOMETIMES...
YOU DON'T NEED A LAWYER!

FREE
TIPS AND TRAPS
to protecting your children, your home and your credit.

NEW!
WITH STICKY NOTE QUICK REFERENCE TIPS!

First Edition
Copyright © 2010 by
Joseph R. "Randy" Klammer, Esq.
All rights reserved.

Clearly Publishing House
6990 Lindsay Drive, Suite 7
Mentor, Ohio 44060

All Rights Reserved

No part of this book may be used, reproduced or transmitted in any form or by any means without the author's prior written permission.

Disclaimer

This book was written with care to provide useful information. The author cannot be responsible for any consequences resulting from using the tips and information in this book. While self-help is empowering and often the only affordable option, there is no substitute for the advice of and representation by an attorney licensed in your jurisdiction. The reader is strongly advised to seek professional advice and assistance when challenged with a legal matter. While the author would welcome the opportunity represent the reader, use or purchase of this book does not create an attorney-client relationship.

Trademark

The "Sometimes...you don't need a..." phrase is a copyright and trademark of the author. Any use or misuse is strictly forbidden.

Readers should feel free to learn more at: www.KLAMMERLAW.com

TABLE OF CONTENTS

Introduction 6

Chapter 1: The court may second guess your parenting decisions. 10

Chapter 2: How dare you speak with my child without me present. 25

Chapter 3: How dare you pat my child down without my permission. My home is my child's castle. 34

Chapter 4: Why can't I just punish my child myself. After all, my parents punished me and I turned out all right. 42

Chapter 5: My kid did what? And I owe how much? 46

Chapter 6: Mom, Dad, and the Department of Job and Family Services. 50

Chapter 7: I'm not a lawyer, how can I make sense of all this. The Constitution to the rescue. 54

Chapter 8: You're protecting your family with a better understanding of Ohio's juvenile justice system, now protect them with a basic will. 58

Chapter 9: Enough. Can't I just disinherit Uncle Sam from my estate. 68

Chapter 10: My kids aside, I still have my own parents to worry about. 71

Chapter 11: I admit I fell behind on my credit card payment, but I'm tired of being pushed around. 76

Chapter 12: Relax. They can't garnish your wages before getting a judgment from court. ... 93

Chapter 13: Falling behind on your mortgage is a different animal. 100

Chapter 14: I'm behind on my rent, but my landlord hasn't fixed a thing I've asked. 113

Chapter 15: My rental unit was perfect, but my landlord won't return my security deposit. 121

Chapter 16: Keep saving on attorneys fees. Small Claims Court allows you to handle a case without a lawyer. 124

Chapter 17: Sure, lawsuits are complicated, but they don't have to be a mystery. 130

Chapter 18: Can't lawyers learn to get along - why all the objections. What do you mean its hearsay...I heard it myself. 139

Chapter 19: Feel the power. 153

APPENDIX OF FORMS 155

INDEX 183

Introduction

There is no debating that lawyering, so to speak, has become a relatively expensive proposition. In a number of regards, the practice of law has become so complicated that it inherently prices itself out of the reach of the average family. The rules of procedure, increased reliance on forensic, medical, and other such scientific evidence, and tightened litigation time frames are just a few of the reasons the practice of law has become more complicated and, hence, more expensive. Fortunately, with tools like the internet and electronic research databases, lawyers can at times find efficiencies in their practices which allow them to advise clients on more run of the mill legal issues in a less costly manner than ever before. Lawyers now have the ability to create *pro forma* documents which might apply to a great variety of clients and hence offer the appropriate associated legal advice at very reasonable fees. Sometimes you may not even need a lawyer.

No place can the advantages created by

technology be more helpful than with more routine legal problems faced by average families. The attorneys at our office, like many I presume, will meet with clients and potential clients and often be presented with rather typical legal questions. Often the answers to the questions are so simple that the client is best advised that it would be most cost effective for the client to handle the matter herself. Handled delicately, the attorney can explain the processes and relevant legal concepts in a manner that empowers the client and avoids leaving the client with the feeling the their trusted attorney has abandoned them. Conscientious lawyers will be careful not to leave the client with the impression that his problems are insignificant; instead, they will walk that client through the process and help the client understand the cost savings associated with self-help.

Because we are confronted with some typical questions on a routine basis, it only seemed appropriate to catalog some of them and some of the more typical advice. I am fortunate to be a very proud member of this legal profession - unfortunately, that also forces me to remind the reader, that no simple guide to such issues can replace advice from a trusted lawyer. That said, this book is written with the realization that too often hiring an attorney may not be a practical option. Hopefully, with the information in this book, some patience and courage on the part of the reader, and careful attention to the details of procedure, the reader can find some solutions to common legal problems that will help protect one's family.

This book is designed to identify some of the more common legal questions and then to explain some of the basic concepts underlying these issues. The explanation will identify various tips and traps to highlight to the reader the presence of certain difficulties and

> Look for these sticky post notes throughout the book for tips and traps

> Use this book with the internet for answers to many of your legal problems.

opportunities. Many of these concepts can be quite complicated. The book addresses the more common issues associated with a variety of topics. **[Tip]** The discussions herein should help the reader better understand certain fundamentals which might guide one to find answers to their problems which might not be addressed in the book itself. The book includes references to the Ohio Revised Code and various citations to cases and secondary materials in footnotes. [1] If hiring an attorney is not an option, use this book along with the power of the internet to find solutions not included herein.

---

[1] This book uses a blended form of citation to aid the reader. Citations to the Ohio Revised Code will appear as "R.C," to United States Supreme Court decisions will appear as "U.S. ," to Ohio Supreme Court Decisions will appear as "Ohio St.," or in an ##-Ohio-#### format, citations to Ohio Appeals Court opinions will appear as "Ohio App." or in a ##-Ohio-#### format.

Chapter 1: The court may second guess your parenting decisions.

It has been said:

"We never know the love of our parents for us till we have become parents."[2]

As the proud father of two young children, I witnessed the truth of this statement at the very instant of the birth of my first born. How powerful and wondrous the parental instinct to sacrifice your welfare and, if need be, your very life for an infant child - whom, as a practical matter, rests in your loving arms as a complete stranger.

I understand now the concern my parents experienced when I failed to return home by curfew or misrepresented to them where I would be on a given evening. Now, I easily imagine the distress when they received my late night telephone call with various excuses for my failure to obey their wishes.

---

[2]Henry Ward Beecher, *Proverbs from Plymouth Pulpit* (1887).

Because of this same experience as a new father, I better understand the distress and confusion experienced by the parents whose child is charged with a juvenile "criminal" offense. What seemed a routine and relatively insignificant criminal allegation to me as a full time prosecutor in the juvenile court, was often confusing and unnerving to the parents of a child so charged. Sure, had these families been represented by an attorney, much of this anxiety could have been alleviated, but many parents viewed the allegations as so insignificant that the expense associated with retaining an expert could not be justified. Only after being snared - often by no fault of their own - by a system they do not understand do parents realize the seriousness of such allegations.

As a parent and an attorney, I am fortunate to understand the unique consequences and liability surrounding children. Their behavior and lack of foresight causes a unique ignorance to the consequences of their behavior. To some degree, this ignorance has forced the law to place much liability upon parents for the uncontrolled actions of their children. Again, good parents too often learn of this potential liability too late to protect themselves and their child.

"In the old days, if a neighbor's apples fell into your yard, you worked it out over the back fence or picked them up and made pies. Today, you sue."[3]

It is true, and many parents can recall their own experiences growing up. There was a time when disputes were settled amicably between complete strangers and children were punished in the home. Today, routinely juvenile behavior, *e.g.* curfew violations, teenage drinking, trespassing, shoplifting and fights between boys at the highschool, result in police investigations, delinquency charges in the juvenile court, courtroom battles and incarceration in the local detention center.

All too often these consequences could have been avoided had the parents been better educated

---

[3]Lee Iacocca, *Talking Straight* (1988), with Sonny Kleinfeld.

about the process and about the various legal issues surrounding the behavior of their children. We, as good parents, learn the specifics about raising our children, but make little if any effort to understand the intricacies of the juvenile justice system and related matters. Knowing just enough to suspect that expert advise is needed, will often prevent unfortunate errors and oversights.

This book should provide insight to various concepts surrounding the behavior of children under Ohio law. Although many of these concepts and principles are ancient, the law always changes and sometimes quite dramatically. Herein, you will learn about concepts of liability and see how it relates to the behavior of your child, as well as the parameters of financial liability resting with parents for the tortuous behavior of their children. With this information, parents will be better prepared to react quickly and prudently to situations when the law involves itself in family.

There is an age old concept in the law known

as the doctrine of *parens patriae* which literally translates "the parent of the country." The concept originates from English common law which allowed the King the royal prerogative to act as the guardians to those with legal disabilities under his rule. Used in this country, the concept allowed the state to act as a child's parent where the child lacks proper care. Today, every state and the federal system have a juvenile justice system.

This system, designed to protect children, allowed the state to make efforts to rehabilitate children where children displayed delinquent behavior, actions which would constitute criminal behavior if committed by adults. The objective of this early system of juvenile justice was to rehabilitate juveniles, so as to protect them from their own misdeeds. The ultimate purpose of this early system was "not to punish, but to save."[4]

---

[4]Flexner & Oppenheimer, *The Legal Aspect of the Juvenile Court* (1922) (Children's Bureau Pub. No. 99.)

The system has continued to grow and change through the decades since its inception. In 1957, one Ohio court of appeals characterized the juvenile system in the state of Ohio as being "in the forefront among the states of this country in the enactment of progressive, humanitarian and benevolent laws for the protection of its children."[5] Reflected therein is evidence of a true dual purpose of the juvenile system, namely to remove criminal tendencies from children so to ultimately protect the community from their adult criminal behavior. In this 1957 opinion, the court explained that the purpose of the system is not "to punish the child, but to take it out of environments, which if continued, would result disastrously to it as well as to society, and thereby create a standing menace to the state[.]"[6]

Nonetheless, there are some statistics that

---

[5]*State v. Miclau* (1957), 104 Ohio App. 347, 352.

[6]*Id.*

suggest the system has failed to correct these potential menaces to the community. A 1997 report indicates that between 1965 and 1990, juvenile arrests for violent crime quadrupled.[7] Unfortunately, most such statistics report only arrests which begs the question as to whether it's the violent behavior or arrests which have risen. Regardless, the 1990s brought with it nationwide demand for new, "get tough" policies in response to juvenile and adult crime. The result: "[p]olicy makers around the nation rushed to legislate the cure."[8]

The legislation that resulted has drastically increased the severity of the potential consequences of juvenile delinquency complaints. Such matters are now more serious, not so much in that the penalties

---

[7] Redding, *Juveniles Transferred to Criminal Court: Legal Reform Proposals Based on Social Science Research* (1997), 1997 Utah Rev. 709, 762.

[8] *State v. Hanning* (2000), 89 Ohio St.3d 86, citing Rossum, *Holding Juveniles Accountable: Reforming America's "Juvenile Injustice System."* (1995), 22 Pepperdine L.Rev. 907.

were changed, but that the entire environment surrounding the system encourages that juvenile delinquents be treated more like their adult counterparts.

In fact, this dichotomy between the treatment and punishment of juvenile delinquents and that of unruly juveniles was the hallmark of Ohio's 2000 Juvenile Justice Reform Act. In essence, the Act recognized and solidified what was truly the reality for years; namely, that because an Ohio delinquent juvenile is subject to a loss of liberty for years, the penalty "is comparable in seriousness to a felony prosecution."[9] Simply stated, "the idealism that created juvenile courts must not be allowed to obscure the fact that a child adjudged delinquent is threatened with a substantial infringement of his liberty."[10] Unfortunately, many parents fail to recognize the

---

[9] *In re Cross* (2002), 96 Ohio St.3d 328, 332, citing *In re Winship* (1970), 397 U.S. 358, 365-366.

[10] *Id.*

potential severity of the delinquency penalties and treat these matters as relatively insignificant.

In fairness, much rhetoric supported this public misconception that juvenile delinquency proceedings were civil - as opposed to criminal - matters. Courts now routinely recognize that such a characterization is to simplistic.[11] The United States Supreme Court has recognized that "[a]lthough the juvenile-court system had its genesis in the desire to provide a distinctive procedure and setting to deal with the problems of youth, including those manifested by antisocial conduct, our decisions in recent years have recognized that there is a gap between the originally benign conception of the system and its realities." *Breed v. Jones* (1975), 421 U.S. 519, 528-529. Unfortunately, someone forgot to explain this reality to parents and their children.

The Ohio Juvenile Justice Reform Act, created an entirely new chapter within the Ohio Revised Code,

---

[11] *Id.*

i.e. R.C. 2152, to exclusively address juvenile delinquency. **[Tip and Trap]** The statement of the purpose of the chapter demonstrates that the law is no longer primarily focused on rehabilitating delinquent children. Rehabilitation of the offender is identified as the fifth and final objective. Instead, the provisions of R.C. 2152.01, *et seq.*, are designed to care for children, protect the public, hold the offender accountable, restore the victim, and ultimately rehabilitate the offender. The reform Act emphasizes that juvenile delinquents must be punished in a manner that is "commensurate with and not demeaning to the seriousness of the delinquent child's" conduct and its impact on the victim.[12]

> Juvenile Court can punish your child with incarceration.

This exact language is found in the provisions which outline the purposes of adult felony sentencing. Oddly enough, the adult sentencing provision places

---

[12] R.C. 2151.01(B).

rehabilitating the offender ahead of restitution to the victim, whereas the juvenile provision places rehabilitating the offender as the last in the list of purposes. True, the stated objectives needn't be viewed in order of importance, but one would surely expect that the drafters of these provision would have taken care to ensure that rehabilitating juveniles remains of distinct importance. One would expect that this paramount objective be immediately apparent to those who look to the statement of purposes for guidance.

This same indistinction is found in the provisions of the Ohio Revised Code which mandate that juvenile delinquent sex offenders are subject to the same sex offender registration requirements as adults. In fact, the juvenile provision specifically references the adult sexual offender registration provisions. These provisions, widely known as "Megan's Law," require that persons classified as a sexual offenders register with the sheriff of their county of residence. The period of registration ranges from ten years to a life long registration requirement.

As with most matters in the law, sexual offender classification and registration is obviously a quite complicated matter. It raises many complicated factual and legal arguments in both the adult and juvenile context. Nonetheless, the mere possibility that a child would be burdened with such a registration requirement should raise the sense of urgency in the mind of any parent with a child rightfully or wrongfully charged with such an offense.

The Juvenile Justice Reform Act in a most unapologetic manner contributed to blurring the distinction between adult and juvenile criminal behavior. The Act specifically implemented what is generally referred to as blended sentencing. Traditionally, the law in Ohio was quite clear, the juvenile court lacks the authority to place a juvenile, regardless of age, in an adult incarceration facility. With regards to incarcerating juveniles, the court was limited to incarceration in the local juvenile detention center or the more restrictive Department of Youth

Services facilities.

With the adoption of a blended sentencing scheme the juvenile courts now have certain discretion to sentence and later impose an adult sentence on juvenile delinquents. The sentences reflect a shift in purpose from rehabilitation of the child to "accountability and punishment."[13] Moreover, that sentence is an "adult sentence" in the truest sense; instead of serving a juvenile delinquency sentence in an adult facility, the court is authorized to order that the juvenile delinquent suffer an adult criminal sentence in an adult jail or prison.

Arguably, this is an overreaction to the public misconception that juvenile violent crime remains on the rise. As the 1999 report of the National Crime Victimization Survey indicates, juvenile crime is on the decline; the proportion of violent offense committed by juveniles has remained steady for the

---

[13] Brandi Moore, Blended Sentencing for Juveniles: The Creation of a Third Criminal Justice System. 22 J. Juve. L. 126, 127 (2001-2002.)

last 25 years.[14] The report also suggests that serious violence by juvenile offenders has dropped 33% between 1993 and 1997.[15] Many commentators argue that the public's mis-perception, caused in part by the media's disproportionate coverage of juvenile violent crime has forced legislators to take a "get tough" approach to juvenile crime.[16]

A public mis-perception or not, the stakes are now markedly higher in juvenile delinquency matters. And, whether or not the system was ever in truth a quasi-civil justice system designed to rehabilitate children, there is no longer any question that the system is criminal in nature and the potential penalties can be life altering. Responsible parents must protect themselves and their children by fully protecting their

---

[14] *Id.*, citing Howard Snyder & Melissa Sickmund, National Center for Juvenile Justice, Juvenile Offenders and Victims: 1999 National Report 89 (1999.)

[15] *Id.*

[16] *Id.*

rights. Understanding the true nature of juvenile proceedings should make the information in the early chapters of this book much more relevant and important to every parent.

Chapter 2: How dare you speak with my child without me present.

At one point or another - hopefully on television as opposed to in real life - we've all heard the damning Miranda warning:

> You have the right to remain silent, that anything you say can be used against you in a court of law, you have the right to the presence of an attorney, and if you cannot afford an attorney one will be appointed for you prior to questioning.

[Trap] To the despair of many parents there is no mention of the right that a parent be present during the questioning of their child, or for the child to request the presence of a parent during questioning.

> Police may interview your child without you present.

This inevitably causes tension when the parents discover that, in their absence, their minor child waived these rights and made a full confession to the alleged crimes. This is even worse when the child made a statement that the police *believe* is a confession.

It does not require any expertise in constitutional law to understand why parents believe their presence is necessary. As care-givers, parents understand that a great portion of their responsibility for their children, is the responsibility to protect their children from themselves. True, few parents actually understand the significance of these constitutional rights, but most recognize that their understanding is weak. Accordingly, many adults reserve their rights so they can speak with an attorney. Children, on the other hand, fail to recognize the significance of their own ignorance.

Unfortunately, for sometime the Ohio Supreme Court has rejected what is known in other states as the "independent advice/interested adult standard," which would require that both the juvenile and his parents or guardian waive these constitutional rights. **[Trap]** Instead, the Ohio Supreme Court has concluded that there is "no requirement in *Miranda* that the parents of a minor shall be read his constitutional rights along with their child, and that, by extension, both parent and child are required to intelligently waive those rights before the minor makes a statement."[17]

[Tip] The Court does requires however that the totality of the circumstances be examined when evaluating whether a confession is voluntary. This totality of the circumstances standard requires that reviewing courts consider all of the circumstances surrounding the confession, including age; mentality; prior criminal experience; the length, intensity, and frequency of the interrogation; the existence of physical mistreatment; and the existence of any threats or inducements.[18] Through this analysis, it is anticipated that courts can properly determine whether the child appreciated and voluntarily waived these *Miranda* rights.

The namesake of these *Miranda* rights is the

---

[17]*In re Watson* (1989), 47 Ohio St.3d 86, 89.

[18]*Id*, at 90.

decision of the United States Supreme Court in a case captioned *Miranda v. Arizona*.[19] The underlying purpose of the decision was to ensure that suspects were fully informed of their constitutional rights. The Constitution and the Bill of Rights provide many powerful rights and privileges. The United States Supreme Court ultimately concluded that a suspect must be first informed of these rights, prior to evaluating whether any waiver of the rights was voluntary.

The United States Supreme Court first recognized that the privilege not to incriminate one's self is a precious right "fixed in our Constitution only after centuries of persecution and struggle."[20] Now in the Constitution, these rights are "secured for ages to come, and * * * designed to approach immortality as nearly as human institutions can approach it."[21]

---

[19] 384 U.S. 436.

[20] *Id.*, at 442.

[21] *Id.*

Despite this grand intention, in practice, this Constitutional privilege was ignored or a waiver was coerced through physical and psychological abuse. The United States Supreme Court quoted Lord Chancellor of England from a 1931 report wherein Lord Sankey described that such abuse is not only criminal, "but involves also dangers of false confessions, and it tends to make police and prosecutors less zealous in the search for objective evidence."[22] Such abuse was, in fact, the state of the art in police interrogation and taught in various police manuals. In the 1960s, when *Miranda* was decided, police manuals on interrogation and confessions instructed that suspects be deprived of "every psychological advantage." The officers were instructed to create an atmosphere which "suggests the invincibility of the forces of the law" where suspects are separated from family and friends whose presence

---

[22]*Id.* at 449, citing IV National Commission on Law Observance and Enforcement, Report on Lawlessness in Law Enforcement 5 (1931).

will lend "moral support."[23]

In this intimidating environment, officers were instructed to employ a number of different interrogation techniques designed to illicit incriminating responses. Officers were instructed to use the classic "Mutt and Jeff" routine thrusting good cop against bad encouraging the suspect to confide in the good. Outright trickery was also encouraged wherein an alleged witness was coached into identifying a suspect from a line up while in the presence of the suspect. Unaware of the trickery, the suspect might offer an incriminating response. Even where the suspect is shrewd enough to invoke the right to remain silent, the officers were instructed to cause "psychological conditioning" by conceding the right, but suggesting the failure to cooperate itself is evidence of guilt.[24]

It was in this context that the United States

---

[23] *Id.* at 449-450.

[24] *Miranda* at 452-454.

Supreme Court concluded that certain safeguards were necessary to ensure that any statement made by a suspect "thrust into an unfamiliar atmosphere and run through menacing police interrogation procedures" is the product of free choice. Obviously, in such an environment, the "privilege against self-incrimination is jeopardized" which necessitates "procedural safeguards" to protect this right. **[Tip]** This procedural safeguard is the "Miranda Warning." The United States Supreme Court directed that an individual in custody be advised of the following:

> He has the right to remain silent, that anything he says can be used against him in a court of law, that he has the right to the presence of an attorney, that if he cannot afford an attorney one will be appointed for him prior to any questioning if he so desires. [25]

---

[25] *Miranda* at 479.

Only after this warning can a waiver of these rights be interpreted as a knowing and intelligent waiver. It is only with a knowing and intelligent waiver that such statements can be used against the suspect. Unfortunately, this same standard is applied to juvenile suspects. There is no requirement that the juvenile be entitled to the advice of a parent or guardian prior to any waiver or that the parent or guardian participate in the waiver. Instead, a court evaluating the waiver will look to the totality of the circumstances, including the juvenile's age, criminal history, and sophistication, to determine whether the child understood the rights and made a knowing and intelligent waiver of said rights.

> A waiver of Miranda rights must be knowing and voluntary.

It is critical that should your child find herself accused of being a delinquent or unruly child - which is the equivalent of being charged with a crime as an adult - that any statements the child may have made be examined against the Miranda rights.

[**Tip**] Should you not be able to afford counsel, your child may be entitled to appointed counsel. Ensure that your child's attorney thoroughly reviews the police reports with an eye toward this analysis. The various rules of procedure require that these issues be raised by written motion at early stages in the proceedings.

> You're child is entitled to a free lawyer.

Chapter 3: How dare you pat my child down without my permission. My home is my child's castle.

There was a time - and may soon be a time again - that law enforcement officers and prosecutors took the position that constitutional privileges that protect adults are not available to children. Although a few remain in debate, most of such constitutional rights are now equally applicable to juvenile proceedings. [26] The Fourth Amendment is one such right; a juvenile's right to be free from unreasonable search and seizure by the government is identical to that of an adult. [27] As is typical, the language of the actual Constitutional Amendment can be difficult to unravel. The Fourth Amendment reads: The right of the people to be secure in their persons, houses, papers,

---

[26] *Davis v. Mississippi* (1969), 394 U.S. 721; *State v. Walls (*2002), 96 Ohio St.3d 437, 446, 775 N.E.2d 829.

[27] *New Jersey v. T.L.O.* (1985), 469 U.S. 325, 105 S.Ct. 733, 83 L.Ed.2d 720.

and effects, against unreasonable searches and seizures, shall not be violated, and no Warrants shall issue, but upon probable cause, supported by Oath or affirmation, and particularly describing the place to be searched, and the persons or things to be seized. The Amendment protects individuals from "unreasonable searches and seizures" by the government in the absence of a warrant issued by a court. The protection has its obvious origins in the concept that one's home is his castle and entitled to the same protections afforded the king's castle. Some trace its origins to a 1600's English case which found that the king's ability to enter the homes of the crown's subjects had certain limitations. The interpretation of the Amendment has become rather complex however. **[Tip]** In simplest terms, a warrant is required to enter a home unless the home is entered for emergency purposes; as a search incident to an otherwise valid arrest; is in hot pursuit of a suspect; is necessary to secure evidence in plain view; or is necessary to secure easily destroyed evidence. These exceptions are generally referred to as an exigent circumstance exception to the warrant requirement. The most obvious of all exceptions to the requirement that a home may only be entered with a warrant, is the consent of the suspect. This will typically be an absolute exception to the warrant requirement allowing a search of the residence.

The Fourth Amendment also protects from an unreasonable search and seizure of the person. As happenstance would have it, one of the landmark cases in defining the limits of an warrantless stop and frisk of an individual originated in Ohio. In *Terry v. Ohio*, the United States Supreme Court ultimately evaluated an officer's decision to stop and search an individual he believed suspicious. A police officer does have the right to stop a person where he can identify "specific and articulable" facts which justify a reasonable suspicion of criminal activity. **[Tip]** The stop should be brief and for the sole purposes of questioning the individual on the suspected criminal activity. Seizure beyond the point necessary to make this inquiry is unreasonable. **[Tip]** The officer can also then conduct a frisk of the person for purposes of identifying a weapon where he can identify a "reasonable suspicion" that the individual is armed and dangerous.[28]

> Police can't just just stop and frisk a person without something more.

This ultimately becomes the difficult aspect of the analysis. Any and all police reports wherein your child may have been subject to a search and seizure without a court order must be analyzed carefully to determine whether a valid exception to the warrant requirement was present. If there is no such exception, the principle known as the "exclusionary rule" requires that the evidenced be excluded or "suppressed" from

---

[28] *Terry v. Ohio* (1968), 392 U.S. 1, 88 S.Ct. 1868.

further proceedings. [29] Interesting, as with *Terry v. Ohio*, the exclusionary rule has its origins in an Ohio dispute, namely *Mapp v. Ohio*.

Of particular significance to children and parents, are school searches. Although children often view their school lockers as their own private property, it is settled that the they are subject to search. **[Tip]** Children have a reduced expectation of privacy in and while on school property; as such, the threshold permitting a warrantless search of your child, her property, or her locker is lowered. [30] The United States Supreme Court in *New Jersey v. T.L.O* explained the law with regards to a search on school grounds best:

> It is evident that the school setting requires some easing of the restrictions to which searches by public authorities are ordinarily subject. The warrant requirement, in particular, is unsuited

---

[29] *Mapp v. Ohio* (1961), 367 U.S. 643, 81 S.Ct. 1684, 6 L.Ed.2d 1081.

[30] *New Jersey v. T.L.O.* (1985), 469 U.S. 325, 341, 105 S.Ct. 733.

to the school environment: requiring a teacher to obtain a warrant before searching a child suspected of an infraction of rules (or of the criminal law) would unduly interfere with the maintenance of the swift and informal disciplinary procedures needed in the schools. Just as we have dispensed with the warrant requirement when 'the burden of obtaining a warrant is likely to frustrate the governmental purpose behind the search,' * * * we hold today that school officials need not obtain a warrant before searching a student who is under their authority.

Ohio has enacted a statute which allows principals to search a child's school locker when criminal activity is suspected. **[Tip]** Section 3313.20 specifically allows school principals to "search any pupil's locker and the contents of the locker that is searched if the principal reasonably suspects that the locker or its contents contains evidence of a pupil's violation of a criminal statute or of a school rule[.]"

> School lockers can be searched with only minimal suspicion.

As with homes and persons, automobiles are also protected by the Fourth Amendment's warrant requirement. This includes a parent's car while driven by a child. That said there are multiple exceptions to the warrant requirement, not the least of which is your child's consent to a search of the car. One of the more common permitted warrantless automobile searches are those made incident to the arrest of the driver of the vehicle. Such searches are valid warrantless searches for weapons or to preserve evidence. [31]

Where the child is arrested for a misdemeanor offense, the analysis is again more complicated. Of significance, Ohio has a statute that actually prohibits an arrest for a minor misdemeanor criminal offense. Section 2935.26 of the Ohio Revised Code prohibits such arrests unless the suspect "requires medical care or is unable to provide for his own safety;" the suspect

---

[31] *Weeks v. United States* (1914), 232 U.S. 383, 34 S.Ct. 341, 58 L.Ed. 652. *Chimel v. California* (1969), 395 U.S. 752, 762-763, 89 S.Ct. 2034, 23 L.Ed.2d 685.

"cannot or will not offer satisfactory evidence of his identity;" the suspect "refuses to sign the citation; or the suspect has previously been cited and failed to appear for the citation."

It may feel inevitable that your child will find himself, rightly or wrongly, in such a position. Should your child be stopped by a police officer, have their person or property searched, or be subject to arrest, it is crucial that the Fourth Amendment protections be evaluated closely.

Chapter 4: Why can't I just punish my child myself. After all, my parents punished me and I turned out all right.

The punishment possibilities for children charged and proven to be delinquent or unruly children in Ohio can be complicated and, at times, much harsher than many parents might expect. Unlike many of the other concepts discussed herein regarding the rights of children, the available punishments are purely statutory. Ohio has a statutory scheme described as the "dispositions" of delinquent or unruly children.

Section 2152.19 of the Ohio Revised Code defines a broad range of possible punishments for delinquent children. By way of example, the broad range of options provided by the statute allows the juvenile court to commit the child to a day camp, detention center or other such institution; may order the child to be subject to probation or intensive probation; may order up to 500 hours of community service for felony level offenses; order the child to be subject to ankle bracelet electronic monitoring; impose drivers license suspensions; and impose financial sanctions and fines.

[Tip] Unlike adult incarceration where the length of the potential incarceration increases with the level of the offense, every level of a juvenile delinquency carriers the same risk of juvenile detention incarceration. Whether a child is determined to be delinquent due to the commission of an offense which would be a misdemeanor or felony if committed by an adult, Section 2152 of the Ohio Revised Code provides a potential for up to 90 days of incarceration in a juvenile detention center. A juvenile detention center is not dissimilar to an adult jail. Typically, the children are assigned a cell similar to those assigned adult offenders, they use common showers, eat at a common cafeteria and share common open space, all very similar to adult jail incarceration.

In addition to incarceration in a juvenile detention center, felony juvenile offenders may be incarcerated with the Ohio Department of Youth Services (DYS). Section 2152.26 of the Ohio Revised

Code provides that a child determined to be delinquent due to the commission of an offense which would be a felony if committed by an adult may be incarcerated with State of Ohio's Department of Youth Service prison system. **[Tip]** In general terms, those offenses which would be felonies of the first and second degree allow incarceration in DYS for a minimum of one year and until the child's 21st birthday. For lower level felonies, the potential DYS incarceration is a minimum of six months incarceration, but not to exceed the child's 21st birthday.

The penalties can be more severe for sex offenses. Ohio now has sexual offender registration requirements for juvenile sex offenders. Ohio adopted a tier system employed by the Federal Adam Walsh Act. Juveniles 14 years or older who commit certain sex offenses will be subject to registration requirements, will have the neighbors notified of the sex conviction, and will have

> Juvenile sex offenders may be required to register for life.

the same publicized on the internet. In general terms, depending on the tier designation, a child may be required to register every year for ten years, every six months for 20 years, or every 90 days for life.

The potential consequences for juvenile offenders are now quite severe. The consequences now reach far beyond the age of 18 - in some instances a child's offense may carry consequences for the remainder of the child's life and bringing with it significant effects on the child's education, career and other quality of life opportunities. As a parent of a child accused of being a delinquent child, it is critical that one understand the significance of these processes and their potential consequences.

Chapter 5: My kid did what? And I owe how much?

Immature decisions by your child can damage a modest family's often carefully balanced finances. **[Trap]** There are a number of instances in Ohio law where a parent can be found financially responsible for the actions of their child. From the simplest perspective, a parent can be liable for the actions of a child where a statute provides such liability; where a parent negligently entrusts a child with a dangerous instrument like a gun or car; or where a parent fails to exercise reasonable supervision or control over a child the consequence of which will probably be injury to another.

> You may be financially responsible for your child's actions in excess of $10,000.00

The Ohio Revised Code has a number of statutes which impose parental liability on parents, and in some instances, also place limits on the amount of that liability. Some of the more common instances are where the child commits vandalism, theft or an assault.

Section 2307.70 of the Ohio Revised Code provides that any person injured due to vandalism, desecration or ethnic intimidation committed by a minor child, may recover up to $15,000.00, costs and attorney fees from the child's parent. Section 3109.09 provides that a parent may be liable up to $10,000.00 where a child willfully damages property or commits a theft offense. Section 3109.10 provides that parents are also liable up to $10,000.00 for a willful and malicious assault by their child.

A parent also has a statutory responsibility for an injury caused by a child's operation of a motor vehicle where the parent endorses the child's driver's license application. **[Trap]** While the significance of the application is often overlooked by the parent, Section 4507.07(B) of the Ohio Revised Code expressly imposes this liability on a parent. It provides that "[a]ny negligence, or willful or wanton misconduct, that is committed by a minor under eighteen years of age when driving a motor vehicle upon a highway shall be imputed to the person who has signed the application of the minor for a probationary license, restricted license, or temporary instruction permit. **Most important, this statute has no cap on the liability as do the provisions for vandalism, theft and assault.**

Even without the express statutory liability resulting from the driver's license application, Ohio case law has always recognized the concept of liability for "negligent entrustment." The concept should be rather self-explanatory. A parent may be liable for a child's wrongful conduct where the misconduct was "within the reasonable comprehension of the alleged negligence of the parents." [32] In other words, a parent will be liable where the "injury committed by the child is a the foreseeable consequence of the parent's negligent act." [33] The instances where this negligent entrustment liability may arise by allowing a child to

---

[32] *American Economy Ins. Co., et al v. Knowles, et al.* (1996), 113 Ohio App.3d 71.

[33] *Nearor v. Davis, et al* (1997), 118 Ohio App.3d 806.

use a car, a firearm, or a power tool.

Certainly, this potential liability should not interfere with a parent's decision to allow their child to grow and learn from mistakes. It would be fair also to say that the law recognizes that a child's actions should be judged against the actions of a child. Nonetheless, a parent is duty bound to recognize the limitations in the judgment and skill sets of children. Most parents recognize this reality for the most important reason that they love their children dearly. Continue to make your decisions so as to protect your child from their own inaction or misconduct. You will also insulate yourself from a great many financial liabilities.

Chapter 6: Mom, Dad, and the Department of Job and Family Services.

Issues of juvenile delinquency, juvenile incarceration and parental liability for a child's actions can be unnerving enough. **[Trap]** Know that in certain instances, the reach of the juvenile court can extend to placing orders on parents. And, in some instances, the court can actually grant protective, temporary or permanent custody to someone other than a parent. In an ideal world, these tools will be reserved for family circumstances presenting the greatest danger to the children.

It is important to understand, however, that our American justice system is an adversarial system based on the presentation of evidence to a neutral fact-finder. Although this system presents the greatest protection and opportunity to the respective parties, it can also place one side at a disadvantage - especially where they are under-skilled, confused or otherwise ill prepared. Nowhere can this inequality be more dangerous than when questions of the abuse, neglect or dependency of a child is at issue.

While juvenile court review of an unruly and delinquent child is typically the result of the actions of the child, review of an abused, neglected, or dependent child is typically the result of action or conditions caused by someone other than the child. A dependent child is in general terms a child who, due to no fault of the parents, is destitute, lives in deplorable conditions or otherwise lacks adequate parental care. [34] A neglected child however is one who suffers similar conditions due to the actions or refusal to act of the parent.[35] Neglect can include a failure to provide subsistence or medical care, or to ensure the child is properly educated. "Education neglect" can be rather common and may arise in instances as common as the excessive school tardiness of the child. It is now also settled that these terms can reach to the child before birth with findings of neglect of an unborn child.

---

[34] R.C. 2151.04.

[35] R.C. 2151.03.

An abused child, however, is something rather different. In general terms, an abused child is a victim of the actions of a parent or caregiver. An abused child is one who suffers physical or emotional injury at the hands of a parent or caregiver. Corporal punishment by a parent will not implicate the prohibition provided the punishment does not amount to an offense of endangering children. In simplest terms, corporal punishment should not amount to abuse unless it carries a "substantial risk of serious physical harm." [36]

Although one might consider "dependent" the least serious category, with neglect next and abused the most serious, the potential case dispositions are essentially the same. If the juvenile court finds any of these conditions to exist, it can make a broad range of orders. The court orders may include: commitment of the child to the protective supervision of the department of job and family services; temporary

---

[36] R.C. 2919.22.

custody to another person; order to follow certain case plans; orders restraining parents or others from engaging with the child; an order to receive certain medical care; and removal of the child from the home. [37] The most extreme order of course is an award of permanent custody which has the legal effect of **permanent termination of a one's parental rights to the child.**

> You may be entitled to a free attorney in abuse, dependency and neglect cases.

It is now well settled that although parents have a fundamental right to raise their children, that right may be terminated. But, because of the significance of this decision, it is settled that parents are entitled to the appointment of counsel provided they can demonstrate that they are otherwise indigent and unable to afford counsel. When confronted with these allegations, it is critical that an attorney be consulted or appointed counsel be applied for immediately.

---

[37]R.C. 2151.353.

Chapter 7: I'm not a lawyer, how can I make sense of all this. The Constitution to the rescue.

There is no better evidence of how beautiful is our system of justice than an indigent's right to appointed counsel. The Sixth Amendment to the United States Constitution provides for the right to counsel. It provides a number of the typical criminal due process rights and specifically provides that an accused has the right "to have the Assistance of Counsel for his defence." The United States Supreme Court in *Gideon v. Wainwright* explained that "the right to the aid of counsel is of this fundamental character." [38] The United States Supreme Court had previously held that the right to counsel is "necessary to insure fundamental human rights of life and liberty." The United States Supreme Court also describes the right to appointed counsel:

---

[38] *Gideon v. Wainwright* (1963), 372 U.S. 335, 83 S. Ct. 792, 9 L. Ed. 2d 799.

From the very beginning, our state and national constitutions and laws have laid great emphasis on procedural and substantive safeguards designed to assure fair trials before impartial tribunals in which every defendant stands equal before the law. This noble ideal cannot be realized if the poor man charged with crime has to face his accusers without a lawyer to assist him. A defendant's need for a lawyer is nowhere better stated than in the moving words of Mr. Justice Sutherland in Powell v. Alabama:

'The right to be heard would be, in many cases, of little avail if it did not comprehend the right to be heard by counsel. Even the intelligent and educated layman has small and sometimes no skill in the science of law. If charged with crime, he is incapable, generally, of determining for himself whether the indictment is good or bad. He is unfamiliar with the rules of evidence. Left without the aid of counsel he may be put on trial without a proper charge, and convicted upon incompetent evidence, or evidence irrelevant to the issue or otherwise inadmissible. He lacks both the skill and knowledge adequately to prepare his defense, even though he have a perfect one. He requires the guiding hand of counsel at every step in the proceedings against him. Without it, though he be not guilty, he faces the danger of conviction because he does not know how to establish his innocence.' 287 U.S., at 68-69, 53 S.Ct., at 64, 77 L.Ed. 158.

For these reasons, indigent criminal defendants and indigent juveniles accused of being a delinquent child are constitutionally entitled to appointed counsel.[39] Ohio has codified this right in Section 2152.351 of the Ohio Revised Code. In fact, the provision also provides that the parent or guardian of the child may be entitled to appointed counsel if they can demonstrate that they are themselves indigent. **[Tip]** Section 2152.351 provides "[a] child, the child's parents or custodian, or any other person in *loco parentis* of the child is entitled to representation by legal counsel at all stages of the proceedings under this

---

[39] *In re Gault* (1967), 387 U.S. 1, 42, 87 S. Ct. 1428, 18 L. Ed. 2d 527.

chapter or Chapter 2152 of the Revised Code. If, as an indigent person, a party is unable to employ counsel, the party is entitled to have counsel provided for the person[.]"

Should you find your child charged as a delinquent child, you should immediately evaluate whether either you, your child, or both are entitled to appointed defense counsel. It is critical that you make this evaluation immediately at the outset of the case. You should immediately contact your local juvenile court to determine whether you are eligible for a court appointed attorney. You should also determine what local rules the court may have relevant to the process of applying for appointed counsel for you and your child. It will be critical that you have the expert assistance of an attorney in evaluating the juvenile delinquency procedures.

[Tip] [Although legal forms are never a substitute for the advice of counsel. You will find useful motions for appointment of counsel and for juvenile discovery in the appendix of forms.]

Chapter 8: You're protecting your family with a better understanding of Ohio's juvenile justice system, now protect them with a basic will.

Providing for your family and particularly your children is every parent's ultimate goal. Your child's welfare is always on your mind. You make many of your decisions daily in your occupation in an effort to better the conditions of your family. With a little planning, one can also ensure that this effort will continue to protect your family should the family suffer an unexpected and tragic death of one or both parents.

Simply stated, there is no way to define how your children should be protected and how your assets should be distributed other than with a document in writing. The most basic of such documents is a simple will. **[Tip]** A will must be in writing. From its earliest definitions, the fundamental purpose of a "will" is a legal declaration of one's intentions which is willed to be performed upon death.[40] A critical element in this definition, however, is that the declaration be a "legal declaration." Ohio, like all other states, has specific statutory requirements for a will to be valid. If these will formalities are not satisfied, one risks the wishes stated in the document to be of no significance.

That said, the will formalities themselves are not overly complicated.[41] **[Tip]** Again, the will formalities change from state to state, but Ohio requires that

> A Will must be written, and signed with two witnesses.

a valid will be in writing, signed at the end of the document, and be attested to by two or more competent witnesses.[42] It is also strongly encouraged

---

[40] Blackstone's Commentaries, 509.

[41] Although an oral will may be valid, it is only permitted in instances of one's last illness. Even then there are certain statutory formalities and writing requirements.

[42] R.C. 2107.03.

that the witness be 18 years of age or older.

With the formalities in place, the document will then define the wishes of the drafter upon death. As such, it is critical that the document be drafted with a great degree of clarity. It will be important that the drafter confirm the correct spelling and full names of all persons to be named in the will and to identify the best possible description of any specific property to be addressed in the will. Often a decedent will leave a bequest to a specific charitable organization, religious institution or other such facility dear to them. **[Trap]** It is not uncommon that the institution will be described in terms common to the local community that are overly loose or colloquial. Unfortunately, at times the colloquial description will have different meanings to different persons, especially when the actual name of the institution is something quite different. It will be critical to confirm the exact official name of the institution and to further identify the same with an accurate street address. With this basic information in place, one can map out her desires.

Where young children are involved, the will can serve an additional purpose of defining whom one wishes to act as the guardian of the person and the estate of the minor child - or adult child for that matter. Typically, the document will define specifically who will act as the guardian of the child and how the child's inheritance will be managed for the child's benefit. The document will also define alternate guardians in the event the primary appointment is unwilling or unable to serve.

Where both parents are living and married, it is important that the parties discuss there respective positions and wishes regarding the care of the children and their inheritance. A typical will also makes provisions in the event both parents die in a common disaster; it will be critical the wishes expressed by the respective parents regarding the care of any minor children be consistent. The contrary would find two wills competing for priority which could create terrible burdens on the survivors. At times, parents will find that a compromise can be reached by separating the guardianship of the child's person from the guardianship of the child's estate. Although this is a relatively common design, it is important the parents consider how well the respective guardians will cooperate to advance the welfare of the child.

Where the parents are separated, the matter becomes much more complicated. In such instances, professional legal advice will be critical. In those instances where communication between the parents is open, a thorough and detailed discussion may identify common ground as well as disagreements. Should the parties find common ground, there certainly may be a method of formulating the document to accomplish these goals. The circumstances of the respective parents, their respective families, and the existing child custody arrangements, will define how complicated is the matter.

With all these matters decided, the document can be drafted. Should one wish to exclude an individual from the will, it is important to give this disinheritance the same amount of consideration. As such, it is critical that the name be accurate; it is also important to detail in the will the reason the individual was disinherited. This will help eliminate the argument that not including the individual must have been an error. With the justification for exclusion explained, the intentional nature of the disinheritance is apparent.

The document itself may be simple but it remains a critical component to protecting one's family. Make it a priority to find some time to talk with your spouse. With some careful discussion, the document can be drafted to accomplish your family's goals.

> Do a power of attorney along with your will.

[Tip] Include with this simple will a health care power of attorney and a living will, and your family will have a reliable estate planning foundation. In fact, many typical estates can be handled adequately with nothing more than these documents. [43] In simplest terms, a "power of attorney" is a document wherein the principal gives the power to another to act in her place. In fact, the simplest definition of an "attorney" is an "agent." A power of attorney can reasonably be viewed as a document which designates another as one's agent on the subjects defined within the document.

A health care power of attorney is a document which grants another the authority to act as the agent for the principal in matters related to health care. The standard form provides that the agent has the authority to make health care decisions when the principal is unable to make the decisions. The authority ranges from selecting medical procedures, hiring and firing medical professionals, authorizing medications, and removing life sustaining treatment.

This document too is rather critical. Should the

---

[43] Again, every family is different and, as such, can present important legal issues. Although it is the author's hope that this guide will provide the reader with valuable information, there is no substitute for consulting with a trusted lawyer.

circumstances arise where a family member is unable to make decisions for herself, the uncertainty created by the absence of a lawful health care agent, can cause additional distress to an already stressed family. The certainty created by this document can eliminate an unnecessary burden and also provide some guidance to the medical professionals themselves.

Unlike the health care power of attorney which gives another the authority to make certain health care decisions, a living will is a directive regarding life sustaining treatment that cannot be reversed by family members. Not to be confused with a "will," a "living will" is in essence a "do not resuscitate" directive by the principal. [44] By executing a living will, the principal directs the physician not to administer or otherwise to withdraw any life sustaining treatment in the event the physician and one other physician

---

[44] The phrase "do not resuscitate order" is not used in this context as it is reserved for that order issued by a physician to carry out the living will wishes.

determine that the principal is in a permanently unconscious state or is suffering from a terminal illness. In this context, the direction to not use life sustaining treatment will include treatments such as simple CPR and artificial nutrition. So, it must be understood that this is very powerful document.

It is also a document which expresses a most personal decision. Many lawyers can share stories about client who mistakenly never executed a living will. After falling into an apparent terminal state, life sustaining treatment was continued only for the purpose of the family to gather for their final thoughts. With families now spread across the nation, by the time the family had gathered the loved one had recovered. Had there been a living will in place, that may not have been the case. Of course, there certainly is no way of knowing, but this just serves as evidence of how significant is the issue underlying a decision to execute a living will.

With the addition of these two documents to the will itself, most estates can be appropriately planned. With a better planned estate, you can continue your efforts as a parent to protect your children and loved ones even after you are living.

[Tip] [Although legal forms are never a substitute for the advice of counsel. You will find useful the *pro forma* last will and testament, health care power of attorney, and living will in the appendix of forms.]

Chapter 9: Enough. Can't I just disinherit Uncle Sam from my estate.

Remember even with a will, Uncle Sam will still get his share of the estate. The executor of the estate may be duty bound to pay to the state of Ohio or the federal government a certain tax, which depends on the value of the estate. From the simplest perspective, the most common assets included in the valuation are bank accounts, stocks or investment accounts, insurance proceeds paid to the estate, cars, boats, and real estate.

> A Will alone can't help you avoid estate taxes.

The rates of taxation have been in constant fluctuation over recent years. As of this writing, Ohio will tax an estate with a net taxable estate of over $338,333.00. The rates of taxation increase as the incremental value of the estate increases. From $338,333.00 to $500,000.00, the rate of taxation is 6% and 7% for those values in excess of $500,000.00.

[Tip and Trap] Although the tax aspect of an

estate can be complicated, it is critical to understand that the will has no effect on taxable nature of the estate. Instead, where there is a concern that the estate may reach a taxable value, it is important to consider other methods of titling property to avoid passing the property through the will. Where the value may reach a taxable value, the estate can use techniques such as payable on death accounts, transfer on death accounts, transfer on death deeds, and outright gifts while living to reduce the net taxable value of the estate below the $338,333.00. Done right, one can then structure the estate to both distribute assets and avoid all or some taxation.

As with the state of Ohio, the federal government has an estate tax structure. In simplest terms, the concepts within the two are quite similar. Although as of this writing, the federal estate tax is repealed for 2010, it will return in 2011. Because of a process known as a "Unified Credit," the effective taxable estate must reach the level of $1,000,000.00 to be subject to taxation in 2011. This has the effect of allowing one to pass up to $1,000,000.00 to heirs without federal estate taxation.

Again, as with the Ohio estate tax, certain techniques can be employed to otherwise protect assets from estate taxation. Should one anticipate that his estate would reach this taxable level, this is one instance where using tools like this book will be of little assistance. In these instances, it will be critical that you discuss the nature of your estate with a trusted attorney to help you protect your family's assets. That said, for those with more humble estates, the estate can be appropriately designed to address asset distribution and estate tax issues with some relatively simple tools. With some careful thought, a simple estate can be designed to protect your family.

Chapter 10: My kids aside, I still have my own parents to worry about.

Being a parent surely brings with it a number of concerns in planning to protect children and the family. Contemporary families often have the responsibility to protect grandparents too. It is almost inevitable that one will be confronted with a situation where their own parents suffer from difficulties in managing their own affairs, be they health, household or financial affairs. Where an elderly parent's condition deteriorates to the level of incompetence, Ohio law has a number of procedures to protect the incompetent person.

Chapter 2111 of the Ohio Revised Code address Guardianships. A "ward" is someone "for whom a guardian is acting" and a "guardian" is a person or association appointed to protect the person, estate or both of a ward. [45] Section 2111.01 of the Ohio Revised Code defines an "incompetent" as a

---

[45] R.C. 2111.01(A) and (B).

"person who is so mentally impaired as a result of a mental or physical illness or disability, or mental retardation, or as a result of chronic substance abuse, that the person is incapable of taking proper care of the person's self or property or fails to provide for the person's family or other persons for whom the person is charged by law to provide, or any person confined to a correctional institution within this state." In simplest terms, the Court will evaluate the condition of the potential ward to determine whether the person suffers from such an infirmity or illness which would make it difficult for the person to protect herself from those inclined to take advantage of her. [46] The Probate Court's focus will be to determine whether it is in the best interest of the prospective ward to appoint another to control the ward's affairs so as to protect the ward from others.

The Probate Court has a broad range of discretion in the conditions and type of guardianship to

---

[46] *In re Guardianship of Corless*, (1981), 2 Ohio App.3d 92.

impose. For instance, the guardianship can be of the person, estate or both; limited guardianship; interim guardianship; or an emergency guardianship. **[Tip]** That said, the Court is obligated to evaluate and ultimately impose the "least restrictive alternative" to a guardianship,

> Anyone can apply to be appointed the guardian of an incompetent person.

namely an alternative which allows the ward to continue to live with liberties most similar to their present circumstances. It is also significant to note that anyone can apply to be appointed the guardian of a person alleged to be incompetent. [47]

> Sign all contracts for the ward as "guardian for."

A guardian has very real responsibilities to be sure that the ward is protected and that decisions are made in the best interest of the ward. Generally speaking, the guardian will not be

---

[47] R.C. 2111.02.

responsible for the debts of the ward so long as any contract entered into is executed with language such as "as guardian" indicating the representative capacity of the guardian. [48] Of course, the duties of the guardian will depend entirely on the nature of guardianship ordered by the Probate Court. For instance, a person appointed as the guardian of the ward's estate is obligated to account for and control the assets of the ward and to manage the same for the ward's best interest. The guardian is also duty bound to make periodic accountings to the Probate Court to evidence the status of the estate. [49]

Unlike a guardian of the estate, the guardian of the person of the ward, is obligated to make living and health care arrangements to best protect the physical welfare of the ward.[50] A guardian of the person has no control of the assets. The expenses incurred in

---

[48] R.C. 2111.151.

[49] R.C. 2111.14.

[50] R.C. 2111.13.

managing the person of the ward will ultimately be paid from the assets of the ward as ordered periodically by the Probate Court. Although typically, the guardian of the person and the estate will be the same person, the Probate Court has sufficient authority to separate the two should that procedure best protect the ward.

That said, unlike a court appointed attorney in criminal or juvenile court matters, there are no procedures allowing for a court appointed attorney to pursue guardianship options. Although the procedures can be rather complicated, they can be understandable with a fair amount of patience. Of course, appropriate legal advice is always ideal, but in those instances where assistance of an attorney is not practical, one should give serious effort to understanding these guardianship procedures where they might provide some protection and security for an infirm family member.

Chapter 11: I admit I fell behind on my credit card payment, but I'm tired of being pushed around.

Certainly, few could deny that many Americans have come to abuse their credit. Some say too often we have confused our wants and our needs. Consumerism has captured the financial lives of many American families. Larry Frank, author of "Wealth Odyssey: The Essential Road Map For Your Financial Journey Where Is It You Are Really Trying To Go With Money?" explains that while other countries also enjoy extraordinary consumption rates, they do not seem to use it as a measure of success. Unlike Americans, other nations also value a healthy savings as a sign of true success.[51] As a result, by the year 2000, Americans had 12% of their annual income in

---

[51] *The Basics: Why Americans Can't Save.* The Christian Science Monitor, http://moneycentral.msn.com/content/Savinganddebt/Savemoney/P145775.asp, July 23, 2009.

credit card debt. [52] In recent years the national savings rate has reached an all time low. According to Philip Nannie, contributing writer for the Washington Business Journal, as of November 2005 "personal savings rate increased nationally to 0.3 percent, meaning that an individual making $40,000 yearly would be saving $120." [53]

Needless to say, we find ourselves in an savings and credit crisis. And, along with credit card abuse it is inevitable that consumers will find themselves under attack by their lenders. Unfortunately, all too often, they've first - and admittedly - fallen behind in their credit card payments. This is all many collection agencies need to justify abusive and demeaning collection tactics.

First, do what you can to ignore these

---

[52] Id.

[53] *Americans Don't Save Enough...And They Don't Care.* Philip Nannie, Washington Business Journal.http://www.bizjournals.com/washington/stories/2005/05/02/focus7.html, July 23, 2009.

collection tactics. Relax. Then take a moment to try to reason through your credit problems and often the "problem" may not be as desperate as you might think.

The first and most powerful tactic in dealing with credit card companies I learned from my dear wife. Now, mind you, my wife is a highly skilled lawyer herself, but the tactic to which I am referring has less to do with her skill as lawyer and more to do with her shear persistence and confidence. Unlike yours truly, she is careful to review all our credit card statements. Whereas I would typical pay what ever "they" claimed was due, she reviews the invoices closely, often calling to challenge a credit card statement late into the evening.

One particular instance comes to mind. In reviewing her credit card statement, the pit bull had noticed that her interest rate had been increased from a 9% to a 15% or so. In a flash, she was on the telephone with

> Stand your ground with credit card companies. Demand documentation.

her bank. Hearing only one side of her telephone conversation, added to my enjoyment of the dialogue. What was obvious was that the justifications they were offering for the rate increase were growing more ridiculous as she was transferred from representative to representative.

After she asked for an explanation for the rate increase, her side of the conversation went something as follows. "Oh, excuse me, but which provision is it in our credit card agreement which allows you to increase my rate due to tough economic conditions...The right answer is, 'there is none.'" After that excuse failed, I heard, "No, I can assure you I was never late on any payment...yes, please do check my payment history. I see, I guess we can agree that I haven't missed any payments." At which point she was placed on hold for a supervisor. What her bank didn't realize was that placing her on hold for 30 minutes was surely not going to deter her - especially in light of the outright lies which they offered as explanations for the drastic rate increase. It was only after we telephoned from another telephone to get to a representative to remind them that my wife was still on hold, did the conversation continue. Of course, at that point they admitted their error and the charges were reversed out. Mind you, this took a good hour of shear doggedness.

If one were to learn anything from these situations it would be that first and foremost, take a moment to give yourself an opportunity to have clarity to think through the problem. **[Tip]** Remember that a credit card contract is like any other contract. The credit agreement defines the terms of the relationship between the parties. Where you are confronted with collection calls that make any demand that causes you discomfort, start first with a request that the credit card agreement and history of payments be forwarded for your review. Have clarity of thought to ask for the documents to which you are entitled. Then take the time to review them for accuracy. You'll be surprised by what you find.

[Tip] Should you find yourself in a position

that the invoicing and other such procedures seem accurate and you are still delinquent, understand that everything in life - even a delinquent tax - is negotiable. Why would that be the case? The answer is simple, pursuing a collection or delaying payment has an expense. Be it the expense for the collection agent or the simple loss of the ability to use the money, every effort to collect a debt has an expense to the credit card company. Hence, the lender has every incentive to try to resolve the matter quickly and in a lesser amount.

This often means that you can resolve a credit card debt for pennies on the dollar. According to Creditinfocenter.com, many of the nation's largest debt purchaser literally will settle debts for 2.4-3.3 cents on the dollar. [54] And often

> Try first to settle for pennies on the dollar...yes, pennies!

---

[54] http://www.creditinfocenter.com/debt/settle_debts.html, July 23, 2009.

you may not be able to settled it for pennies dollar, but nickels, dimes or quarters wouldn't be so bad either. That said, the dialogue will never start if you don't make a proposal. As with the clarity of thought and confidence to challenge the billing, you must have the confidence to make an offer that amounts to pennies on the dollar - if you don't ask, you'll never know. Relax. Be comfortable with the discussion you are about to have and never feel pressured to resolve the matter in one telephone call.

[Trap] Understand too that there are tax consequences associated with a credit card debt forgiveness. As we'll see again in the discussion about mortgage delinquencies below, it is absolutely critical to understand this tax consequence. In simple terms, the bank forgiveness will be reported to the IRS by the bank as a discharge of indebtedness. The lender will then file a 1099 with the IRS which places the burden on the debtor to explain why no tax is due. The simplest and most common exemption from taxation in these circumstances is where the debtor is insolvent prior to the debt forgiveness. But the exemption is only applied to the level of insolvency. In other words, you will have to pay on any amount in excess of your insolvency, or in simpler terms your net worth. **[Tip]** I have experienced instances in my practice where the tax consequences from the debt settlement would have actually cost the debtor enough that client's accountant recommended paying more on the debt than we had negotiated.

There are some topics where professional advice is quite important. The taxes consequences of debt settlement are simply inappropriate for any basic legal guide. The best and most honest advice is to discuss the matter with your lawyer or accountant. Again, this book may work best with certain internet resources. In this instance, the www.irs.gov has a variety of useful information.

> Don't be pressured by a collector's threat of a deadline. They are rarely true.

In all my experience dealing with clients with

both small and large debt problems, I have never experienced a situation where the debtor's deadline has ever been real. Rarely believe a bill collector's threat that the offer will only be open until the end of the phone call, day, or week. Not only are these threats rarely true, you should never make such a decision under any feeling of duress. Understand, that if you don't agree to pay the debt, the lender can only collect by filing a lawsuit against you. Although that can often be a frightening concept, understand that the processes will often offer you an opportunity to continue to review the matter - and most important - to continue to enter into settlement negotiations. Generally speaking, the economies remain the same after a lawsuit is filed as when the debt collector is calling; there continue to be expenses to pursue collection and this can work to your practical advantage. **[Tip]** Again, however, relax and think through the process.

Before you pay, remember **DON'T**:

- **D**   Did you get the **D**ocuments to prove the debt, namely the invoice and credit card agreement.
- **O**   **O**nly pay what you are comfortable they've proven you owe.
- **N**   **N**ever, ever feel pressured to agree.
- **T**   **T**ime can be your ally. Don't feel pressured by a debt collector's threatened deadlines.

Should you be unable to resolve the matter, understand that there are a great number of consumer protection laws in the state of Ohio. One landmark consumer protection statute was the Federal Fair Debt Collection Practices Act. Congress enacted the Act in response to a finding that there was abundant evidence of abuse, deception and unfair practices by debt collectors and this has contributed to a great number of personal financial tragedies. The FDCPA has a number of prohibitions which will be evaluated from the perspective of "the least sophisticated consumer."

[55] This standard will protect "the gullible as well as the shrewd."

Looking at the Act from a basic perspective, it first requires that certain notices be provided the debtor. One such notice is the debt validation notice which effectively indicates

> Demand proof from the collector and all collection efforts stop until proof is provided.

if the debt is not disputed it will be presumed accurate. **[Tip]** This is significant to you as the debtor because the FDCPA requires that if the debtor disputes the debt, all collection efforts must cease until the debt collector confirms the debt with the lender. [56] Moreover, the debt collector may not use language that might confuse the debtor as to his rights for debt validation. Bold, colored print language demanding immediate payment, "call us now," or other such

---

[55] *Clomon v. Jackson* (1993), 988 F.2d 1314.

[56] 15 U.S.C.A. § 1692g(b).

language may very well violate the Act.

One other more relevant provision of the FDCPA provides that a debt collector may not threaten action that is not authorized or is otherwise illegal. [57]

[Tip] One common, but illegal, collection tactic is to threaten litigation within a certain period which is not authorized by the lender and the lawsuit is not filed. When confronted by this threat, a simple request that the collector confirm that the threatened litigation is authorized may be enough to balance out some of the inequities in the negotiation. Another common tactic is to threaten a lien or garnishment when the same can only be accomplished after a lawsuit, judgement, and notice of any such collection effort post-judgment.

> Don't let them threaten a lien. They need to file a lawsuit and win first.

Often it's the shear volume of calls that cause

---

[57] 15 U.S.C.A. § 1692e(5).

the debtor the most discomfort. The FDCPA also addresses this type of abuse. It prohibits "any conduct the natural consequence of which is to harass, oppress, or abuse any person in connection with the collection of a debt." [58] Some of the more typical tactics which violate the anti-abuse provision include excessive telephone calls, telephone calls at the debtors place of employment, abusive or foul language, and telephone calls where the collector either misrepresents or refuses to provide an identity. **[Tip]** The Act also prohibits communications which the collector knows to be inconvenient to the debtor or before 8:00 AM and after 9:00 PM.

Understand, that these federal debt collection protections also include statutory penalties and other such remedies. A debtor only has one year however to bring any action against a debtor or debt collector for an alleged violation of the Act. [59] Although the

---

[58] 15 U.S.C.A. § 1692d.

[59] 15 U.S.C.A. § 1692k(d).

compensatory damages aspect of the Act only allow recovery for "actual damages" resulting from a violation of the Act, the Act does allow recovery for embarrassment, humiliation, and emotion distress. The Act also allows up to $1,000.00 in statutory damages and attorney fees regardless of the amount of actual damages. [60]

Not only will these actions by debt collectors implicate the federal Act, they may also implicate Ohio's Consumer Sales Practices Act. In fact, the Ohio CSPA is arguably broader than the FDCPA in that the federal Act only applies to debt collectors while the Ohio Consumer Sales Practices Act will include actions by both debt collectors and the original lender. As with the FDCPA, the Ohio Act provides for statutory damages of the greater of $200 or three times the actual damages and attorney fees. [61]

---

[60] 15 U.S.C.A. § 1692k(a)(2), 15 U.S.C.A. § 1692k(a)(3).

[61] R.C. 1345.09.

Although there a great number of consumer protection provisions provided by state and federal law, a basic understanding of the Federal Fair Debt Collection Practice Act and the Ohio Consumer Sales Practices Act will help you prepare yourself to evaluate the claims of your lender and its debt collector. It would be impossible for any basic legal guide to address all of these laws and their various provision. But, a basic understanding of the FDCPA and the Ohio CSPA, along with the confidence to raise these issues with the debt collectors may help you alleviate some of the anxiety associated with the collection efforts themselves. This in turn may allow you and your family to better understand the debt and to better prepare a position toward resolution of any legitimate delinquency.

Should you not be able to find a resolution of the alleged delinquency by way of negotiation, there will likely be a lawsuit filed against you. The basics of a lawsuit and a trial and some important tips are included in later chapters of this guide.

There is one important point that is particularly relevant to lawsuits on credit card debts. Remember that all complaints filed to collect on an account must include a statement of the account attached to the complaint. [62] Such an account must include the name of the party and generally have a starting sum of $0.00 or some other amount that is otherwise provable. It must then have dated and identified items of credit and debit so as to allow the court to calculate the balance due. [63]

Remember also that many of these credit card debts are pursued not by the original creditor, but instead an entity that purchased the debt from the original creditor. This is a critical point to consider. The purchaser will then have the obligation of proving a valid agreement assigning the debt. [64] If the plaintiff

---

[62] Ohio Rule of Civil Procedure 10.

[63] *Asset Acceptance Corp. v. Proctor* (2004), 156 Ohio App. 3d 60.

[64] *Zwick & Zwick v. Suburban Construction Co.* (1956), 103 Ohio App. 83.

cannot demonstrate that such a valid agreement exists, the lawsuit should fail as the plaintiff is not the real party in interest.

Do not take the affidavit of an alleged records custodian as sufficient evidence. Plaintiff creditors often argue that the existence of the assignment is a business record and testimony to that fact is an exception to the hearsay rule as discussed in later chapters. Although there do not appear any Ohio cases on the issue, there is a strong argument that the existence of the debt itself is not a business record. Read closely the discussion about the business record exception to the hearsay prohibition found in the later chapters. The plainest argument is that the debt assignment simply does not document a regularly conducted business activity as required by Ohio's evidentiary rules.

With that understanding and the practicalities of negotiation discussed above, you can prepare yourself to defend the attacks on your billfold.

Chapter 12: Relax. They can't garnish your wages before getting a judgment from court.

One of the most common questions asked by clients that find themselves behind on certain debt obligations is whether their wages will be garnished. Relax.

> They can't garnish until they sue and win.

When it comes to garnishment of wages, it cannot be done without a court judgment.

In Ohio, there are two forms of garnishment, one for garnishment of earnings and one for garnishment of other than earnings, which is generally referred to as an "other than" garnishment. As most people that find themselves struggling to pay credit card debt have little other than their earnings, i.e. their wages, garnishment of wages is the most common concern. The reason for this concern is obvious; most of these families are struggling paycheck to paycheck. Should they suffer the loss of a paycheck by garnishment, many necessities will be sacrificed. Eliminating necessary expenses from a family budget can have a very real effect on the health of the family.

Again, a court ordered judgment is required prior to garnishment. This requires that the creditor, for instance the credit card lender, file a lawsuit and that the matter be processed until the court grants the creditor a judgment against the debtor. As we learned above, the lawsuit can also be viewed as another opportunity to negotiate a resolution. Remember though, should one negotiate a resolution which grants the creditor a judgment, that judgment may be the basis of a garnishment of wages at some later date.

Only when the judgment is granted may the garnishment proceed. The garnishment of wages will begin with the creditor issuing a 15 day demand for payment to the debtor. If that goes unanswered, the creditor will file a document known as a creditor's affidavit, wherein the creditor or its attorney swears to the court that it has a judgment and that there is good cause to believe the debtor has earnings.

At this point, the debtor begins to lose more control over the process. The court will serve the employer, who becomes the garnishee, with documents known as the garnishment order, garnishment notice, and an answer form. The order and notice place the employer on notice of its duty to withhold monies from the debtor's paycheck and to forward them to the court. The answer form requires the employer to explain to the court the status of the debtor's earnings.

Within five days of receipt, the employer must serve the debtor with the notice to judgment debtor and the judgment debtor's request for a hearing. The request for a hearing is a critical document. If you are served with such a document, you have five days within which to request your hearing. If you don't request a hearing on the garnishment, your objections to the garnishment are considered waived.

> Don't forget to object to garnishment. Otherwise it's a waiver.

The request for a hearing must state specific

reasons why the wages are exempt from garnishment. The exemptions can be found in Section 2329.66 of the Ohio Revised Code. The most common exemption to a wage garnishment is that wages in the amount of 75% of the debtor's disposable income are protected.[65]

> Like I said, immediately contest garnishment and the underlying judgment.

If this notice of garnishment is the first you are learning about the lawsuit, it will be critical that you immediately attack the underlying judgment. The most common tool to reopen the underlying litigation is a motion for relief from judgment. The permissible reasons for such a motion are identified in Rule 60 of the Ohio Rules of Civil Procedure. Often, service of the lawsuit will have been perfected on the

---

[65] R.C. 2329.66(A)(13) specifically indicates the greater of a certain minimum wage calculation or the disposable income threshold. Depending on the circumstance of the debtor, it will be important to consider both.

debtor by certified mail to an old address or to a former spouse. In such instances, although service may be technically sufficient, the debtor may actually never have been made aware of the lawsuit and the matter will be taken to judgment. The debtor is then surprised to learn about not only the judgment but the wage garnishment.

It is critical to immediately attempt to attack the underlying judgment. **[Tip]** Even in instances where the debtor is aware of the judgment, requesting a hearing on the garnishment, may provide an opportunity to negotiate a wage garnishment in an amount that may provide some relief that the statutory amount of garnishment will not provide. Take advantage of the opportunity to request a hearing and begin a dialogue with judgment creditor on this issue if garnishment is a foregone conclusion.

Other than garnishment of earnings, judgment debtors may garnish assets such as savings and checking accounts. If the creditor doesn't know where specifically the debtor does her banking, the creditor will often issue a blanket set of garnishments and focus on some of the more likely banks in the area. Should the garnishment find a bank where the debtor holds an account, the garnishment will immediately attach that account.

The process of garnishing bank accounts is distinct from wage garnishment in one important way. **[Trap]** Pre-notice garnishment of bank garnishment is not required as it is in wage garnishment. From the creditor's standpoint, the reason is obvious: the debtor would immediately remove the funds from the account.

As with most topics in this guide, its not possible to address all issues that arise with garnishments. The most common issue that arises with a bank garnishment is tracing the monies in the account to an otherwise exempt source. For instance, the monies deposited from earnings may be partially exempt as described above. The monies don't lose their protection because of deposit into a checking account.[66] Some of the other more common exempt monies are unemployment compensation, some workers compensation monies, and certain child support or alimony monies necessary for a person or her dependents.[67]

Those debtor related garnishment issues aside, there are some common creditor related garnishment issues that do arise. Keep the above concepts in mind and you will do much better in defending your assets.

---

[66] *Daugherty v. Central Trust Co. of Northeastern Ohio* (1986), 28 Ohio St.3d 441.

[67] R.C. 4141.32, 4123.67, 2329.66(A)(11).

Chapter 13: Falling behind on your mortgage is a different animal.

While credit card delinquencies can typically be negotiated to pennies on the dollar, mortgage obligations are a different animal all together. The most striking difference between a home loan and a credit card debt is that a home loan is secured by a mortgage. A credit card debt is typically an unsecured debt obligation, which means that the credit card company essentially lives or dies along with your financial health. A home loan however is different in that the loan is secured by a mortgage on the home. If the bank does its job estimating the value of the property as against the loan obligation, it will ensure there is an asset with enough value to guaranty the loan will get repaid. There are numerous explanations for the current mortgage and home value crisis our nation is experiencing, but suffice it to say that banks in general fell into a bad habit of overestimating present and future home values. This in turn allowed them to lower the threshold at which they would lend to homeowners. When home values failed to sustain or live up to the expectations of the banks, the bank as lender lost the asset which was so critical to the security of the loan.

This reality also presents an opportunity for homeowners who find themselves in mortgage delinquency or foreclosure. Understand first, that although a bank may have a mortgage security, the process by which it will foreclose on the mortgage interest is, generally speaking, like any other lawsuit. The bank will need to file a complaint, you will have the opportunity to answer, and argue important issues through motion practice. Understand at least the fact that this process

> Try to relax. Remember a foreclosure is like any other lawsuit. You have notice and an opportunity to respond. Make sure you respond to every pleading. And request a hearing in writing if you don't think the bank is playing straight.

gives you some time before the home is auctioned upon foreclosure.

This extra time, combined with the low home values, may allow you to communicate with your bank and discuss various alternatives to foreclosure. Unlike a credit card debt, however, don't expect to negotiate and stay in your home for pennies on the dollar.

Probably the most important rule is to pay your mortgage first. Should your family find itself in a position that it cannot pay all its debts, be sure to pay for your shelter and food first. If you can't pay your entire mortgage be sure to pay as much as truthfully possible. Not only will partial payments typically slow the bank's decision to file for foreclosure, it shows good faith on your part to both the bank and the court. Your partial payments will also serve to support any arguments you might make to lower your monthly payment.

After you are sure that you are giving your mortgage obligation priority over the rest of your debt obligations, it is also critical to communicate with your bank. Understand this much: keeping your desperate financial condition secret from your bank will serve no purpose. First, the bank will obviously learn of your troubles when you make delinquent or partial payments. And, should a foreclosure be filed, your financial health will be even more obvious. Accordingly, communicate with your bank as early as possible in the process.

An early dialogue with the bank may even allow you to defer all or a portion of your payments or start the process to lower your obligation all together. This brings us back to the importance of understanding that the bank carries certain risk due to the lower home values. In simple terms, a bank is in the business of receiving investments in the form of savings and the like, investing those monies elsewhere, including in home loans, and securing its investment by certain tools, including mortgages. In short, the bank hopes that it can pay you two, three or four percent on deposits like savings or certificates of deposit and then use your monies to invest in opportunities like home loans which will pay back to the bank interest five, six, seven or more percent. [68] Remember also that the bank uses a similar process when it issues credit cards. But, unlike a home loan, the credit cards we've learned are unsecured. Hence, the interest rates charged on credit cards are nine to sometimes in excess of 25 percent. The rates on credit cards are obviously higher because they are not secured by a mortgage; there is much greater risk to the bank. The bank however is supposed to have smarter economists than the borrower. It is expected to make a calculated decision that in the long run they will make more on these loans then they will pay you on your savings.

As regarding mortgage delinquencies, your best negotiating tool is the present state of home values. Understand that if the bank takes the property

---

[68] This is obviously a highly simplified explanation of the business of a bank, but is should serve the point.

104

back or sells during foreclosure, it is stuck with the same value that you would see in the market. Hence, if you can present to the bank a proposal that makes more financial sense than the bank owning the property or selling at auction, there is a possibility to resolve the foreclosure.

The first obvious option would be to propose to the bank a refinancing that would lower your obligation. **[Tip]** This will require a great amount of dialogue, so it is important that you start this process early. Not only can banks be rather impersonal, but with the home value crisis, banks are overburdened with refinancing applications. So, start early and be prepared to provide the bank evidence of all your family's income and debt obligations. That said, the ultimate decision rests with the bank, so be both truthful and diligent in answering all the bank's questions.

This can be important for another reason. Should a foreclosure lawsuit be filed, you want to be able to demonstrate to the court your efforts to resolve the matter. Along with banks, courts are now burdened by the great volume of foreclosure cases. It should be a fair estimation that the court will prefer the parties resolve a case without additional court time where possible. If you can demonstrate your good faith and reasonableness with actual documentation, you can shift slightly the burden to the bank to demonstrate why there is no other possibility but litigation. Accordingly, it is important to continuously communicate with the bank in writing and to keep a copy of everything you send.

If you want your family to have the ability to stay in the property, you should understand two important concepts, namely "forbearance agreement" and "loan modification." Typically, in the foreclosure context, the forbearance agreement and the refinancing work together. A forbearance agreement is an agreement between you and the bank wherein the bank agrees not to pursue foreclosure, so long as you stay on a certain payment plan. Generally, it will cover a period necessary to allow you to apply for loan modification. A loan modification is relatively straight forward, it is the process where the bank will consider new loan obligations, including lengthening the term of the loan, modifying the interest rate and possibly a different type of loan.

At this stage of a homeowner's distress, the loan modification will generally be handled with the bank's loss mitigation department. In simple terms, that department is charged with evaluating the best method of lessening the losses to the bank - do not assume this department has your interest at heart.

Unlike a loan modification and if you are prepared to sacrifice the home, your primary concern must be protecting your credit score. When you've reached this stage, it is important to understand the concept of a short sale. The process of "shorting" an asset is an investment strategy wherein an investor would borrow an asset from another and then sell it. The process is profitable if the asset drops in price so the investor can repurchase the asset with sufficient time to return it from whom it was borrowed. The investor would then profit on the difference of the sale price and the lower price at which it was repurchased.

In general terms, the process of shorting is buying high and selling low - as opposed to the traditional strategy of buying low and selling high. In the context of the a short sale to avoid a foreclosure, the bank benefits by avoiding the expense associated with foreclosure.

A short sale typically does not allow the delinquent borrower to remain in the home; instead, it offers the borrower the flexibility to list the home for sale with the understanding that the bank will accept a purchase price that is less than the loan amount secured by the mortgage. For instance, if one owes $200,000.00 on a home loan which is protected by a mortgage security and is unable to the make the payments, it becomes a crisis when the fair market value of the property falls below the $200,000.00. In such a situation, the homeowner is quite restrained in that it cannot contract to sell the property for less without sufficient funds to pay the bank the entire $200,000.00 owed.

If, for instance, the property has a fair market value of $175,000.00 and the borrower can find a willing buyer for that amount, the bank will need to consent to this lesser amount. This is a short sale. The borrower will need to coordinate with the bank and acquire the consent to the short sale. In which case, the buyer would buy at $175,000.00; the bank would take $175,000.00 on the $200,000.00 owed, and the borrower would walk away from the $200,000.00 obligation. But, remember, the homeowner would also lose the home; nonetheless, the heavy loan obligation would be eliminated.

[Trap] That said, as with credit card debt discussed previously, there are tax consequences associated with a short sale. It is absolutely critical to understand this tax consequence. The transfer of the property is a taxable event. The treatment of the income received from this event is quite complicated. In simple terms, the $25,000.00 bank forgiveness will be reported to the IRS by the bank as a discharge of indebtedness. The lender will then file a 1099 with the IRS which places the burden on the homeowner to explain why no tax is due. The simplest and most common exemption from taxation in this instance is where the sale was for the homeowner's principal residence, in which case, the income is generally not taxable.

That said, it truly is not appropriate for any basic explanation. The best and most honest advice is to discuss the matter with your lawyer or accountant. Again, this book may work best with internet resources. In this instance, the www.irs.gov has a variety of useful information.

Similar to a short sale, a deed in lieu of foreclosure will help a borrower avoid foreclosure and may provide some protection to the homeowner's credit rating. Similar to a short sale, the bank is agreeing to release all or a portion of the loan obligation in exchange for some lesser value. Unlike a short sale, in a deed in lieu, the homeowner is actually transferring the deed back to the bank and the bank is accepting it in lieu of pursuing a foreclosure lawsuit - hence the reference to a "deed in lieu of foreclosure." A deed in lieu of foreclosure implicates the same taxation concerns described above.

The long and short of this discussion is that there are options when faced with a growing mortgage delinquency. Again, it is critical to give the mortgage obligations priority in your household obligations. When the delinquency is unavoidable, it is critical to begin a dialogue with your lender. Be sure that the bank's loss mitigation considers all the various options, including loan modification, short sale and deed in lieu. Specifically, ask the loss mitigation specialist to explain - and explain in terms you can understand - why the other options are not practical.

With some patience and confidence, you may be able to find a solution that is both most helpful and comfortable for your family. Understand from the outset that the process is quite stressful, but the alternative of foreclosure is even more so. Relax to give yourself time to think clearly. Then follow the advice above to patiently unravel the situation to best protect your family.

Chapter 14: I'm behind on my rent, but my landlord hasn't fixed a thing I've asked.

Disputes between landlords and tenants can be some of the more common that result in a lawsuit. This is so for the simple reason that a landlord must file a lawsuit to forcibly evict a tenant from a premises. That said, as streamlined as an eviction might appear, the various rights and duties of the landlord and tenant can be rather complicated. As with the other topics in this book, landlord-tenant disputes can be complicated. This chapter will focus on the more common disputes between the parties and hopefully provide the reader some easy answers. Most often, the parties will dispute the landlord's duty to make repairs, the tenant's duty to maintain the premises and the appliances, the tenant's ability to withhold rent, and the eviction process itself.

A residential landlord-tenant relationship is really unlike most other relationships in the eyes of the law. For the most part, regardless of the agreement of the parties, the Ohio Revised Code will place very explicit duties on the landlord. Although there are also statutory duties of the tenant, it is simpler to understand that the statutes impose more obligations on the landlord. The law presumes that the landlord will be in a more powerful bargaining position. Because having shelter is so critical, the law tries to level the inequities to protect the tenants.

Again, if you only had a moment to learn a few landlord-tenant concepts, focus on the landlord's duty to repair; the rights of a tenant to withhold rent; and the procedures surrounding the return of a security deposit. **[Tip]** Section 5321.04 of the Ohio Revised Code is titled "Obligations of Landlord," and it outlines a number of explicit statutory obligations of the landlord. Subsection (A)(1) requires that the landlord comply with all building code and health department requirements; (A)(2) requires the landlord to make all repairs so as to keep the premises fit and

> Landlord's duty to repair and comply with building codes.

habitable; and (A)(4) requires the landlord to keep all mechanical system, water, and heat systems, and appliances in good and working order. This duty to repair has its origins in case law, referred to as common law. The duty is so strong that even if the condition is defective at the start of the tenancy, the landlord is obligated to make the repairs.[69] If the landlord fails in this obligation, the tenant may terminate the relationship immediately.

Interestingly, common problems such as bug infestation may amount to a violation of the duty to maintain or otherwise amount to a "constructive eviction" of the tenant.[70] Likewise, a cockroach infestation may violate the landlord's duty to maintain the premises.[71] There is also some argument that an excessive mold problem may amount to a

---

[69] *Miller v. Ritchie* (1989), 45 Ohio St. 3d 222.

[70] *Katz v. Comisar* 1930WL2858.

[71] *Harpel, et al. v. Pierce*, 1999WL55700.

constructive eviction if the tenant can relate the mold to a health condition with appropriate expert testimony. [72]

Although a tenant has certain obligations not to damage the premises, the statute does not obligate the tenant to make repairs. Section 5321.05 of the Ohio Revised Code outlines the tenant obligations. **[Trap]** In general terms, the statute provides that the tenant shall protect the property and not allow it to be defaced or damaged, and to use the mechanical systems and appliances appropriately to protect them from damage. This tenant duty not to damage the property, may however eliminate the landlord's duty to repair if the needed repair is the result of damage by tenant. Not only does the statute allow the landlord to sue for damages, the tenant's failure to maintain the property will allow landlord to terminate the lease agreement. [73]

---

[72] *Bogner, et al. v. Titleist Club, LLC, et al.*, 2006-Ohio-7003.

[73] R.C. 5321.05(C).

A typical landlord-tenant dispute will find a landlord suing for eviction for non-payment of rent with the tenant responding with complaints about a failure to repair. Regardless of whom initiates the dispute, the two complaints of failure to repair and failure to pay rent are often part of the same dispute.

> Tenants can't just withhold rent. There are specific statutory requirements for rent withholding.

The Ohio Revised Code is rather clear on these issues. Although, case law may be necessary to interpret the statute's use of "reasonable time" as referenced in R.C. 5321.07(B). That section requires the landlord to repair within the shorter of 30 days or "within a reasonable time." Section 5321.07 outlines clearly the tenant's remedies for a landlord's failure to satisfy a statutory duty. [74] **[Trap]** Simply withholding rent is not a straight forward option. Per

---

[74] *Stiffler v. Canterbury Runn Apartments* 2002-Ohio-5382; *National City Bank v. Fleming* (1981), 2 Ohio App.3d 50, (addressing "reasonable time" as used in R.C. 5321.07.)

Section 5321.07, prior to withholding rent, a tenant must provide a landlord written notice of the alleged violation of a landlord duty. If the landlord fails to remedy the condition within the sooner of a reasonable period in light of the nature of the condition or 30 days, then the tenant may deposit rent with the municipal court, apply for a court order directing the landlord to make the repairs, or terminate the rental agreement.[75] The rent escrow deposit is rather simple and many courts will have a standard form for rent escrow. Typically, one will need the written notice to the landlord, the actual rent check deposit, and filing fees.

If the dispute has gone this far, one would assume an eviction has been filed or one is inevitable. A residential eviction must start with the filing of a notice described as a "three day notice." Chapter 1923 of the Ohio Revised Code outlines the procedures for eviction, also known as "forcible entry and detainer." The three day notice must explain to

---

[75] R.C. 5321.07(B)(1),(2), and (3).

the tenant that an eviction will be filed if the premises are not vacated within three days. Although there is specific statutory language that is required, most three day notice forms are boilerplate and rarely is the language missing.

That said, service of the three notice is at times an issue. And the failure to adequately serve the three day notice will result in dismissal of the eviction. Although, mind you, that

> Don't ignore an eviction lawsuit. Respond with all your tenant complaints in writing to the court.

does not prevent a landlord from again serving the notice in an appropriate fashion and then refiling the eviction complaint. Although notice can be accomplished by certified mail or hand-delivery to the tenant, most are served by leaving a copy of the three day notice taped to the door of the rental unit.

If the tenant fails to vacate, an eviction complaint will be filed. It will be important to immediately evaluate that complaint and be prepared to respond and present any counterclaims. The basics of a lawsuit will be discussed later. Although the time frames in an eviction case are shortened, the principles otherwise applicable to civil lawsuits generally apply equally to an eviction case. Again, as the landlord's failure to maintain the premises is a typical tenant complaint, that claim must be stated in a counterclaim to the eviction complaint. If the landlord has continued to accept rent after the filing of the eviction complaint, that must also be stated and may be a complete defense to the eviction. [76]

As with every lawsuit, an eviction complaint must be taken seriously. It will be critical that you immediately review the complaint and be prepared to state your position in response. Leaving the matter unaddressed will only result in an eviction. The loss of a home can be devastating to your family's welfare and your credit rating. As such, it must be handled as a priority.

---

[76] *Colber v. McLemore* 2003-Ohio-3255; *Associated Estates Corp. v. Bartell* (1985), 24 Ohio App.3d 6.

Chapter 15: My rental unit was perfect, but my landlord won't return my security deposit.

There is probably no more common a dispute between a landlord and tenant than that about the return of security deposits. First, understand that any security deposit in excess of the greater of $50.00 or one month's rent, must earn interest at 5%. [77] Upon the termination of the rental agreement, the landlord may charge against the security deposit for past due rent and for repairs beyond normal wear and tear. [78]

[Tip] That said, within 30 days of the termination of the rental agreement, the landlord must provide a written itemization of the damages to the tenant and return to

> Provide the landlord your new address. The landlord must itemize damages and return remainder of security deposit.

---

[77] R.C. 5321.16(A).

[78] R.C. 5321.16(A).

the tenant the unused portion of the security deposit.

[Trap] Section 5321.16(B) of the Ohio Revised Code also provides that the landlord has no obligation to the tenant if the tenant fails to provide notice of the tenant's new address. If the new address is provided and the landlord fails to provide the itemization and the remainder of the security deposit, a tenant is entitled to statutory damages in the amount of two times the wrongfully withheld security deposit plus any attorney fees incurred.

> Court may order two times deposit that should have been returned.

An important aspect of this statutory damages provision is that it may only be calculated against the amount wrongfully withheld. If the landlord can present evidence of damages to the premises beyond normal wear and tear, the cost to make those repairs will be credited to the landlord. As such, it is crucial that you first appropriately maintain the premises and then, upon termination of the tenancy, take detailed photographs of the condition of the premises. These photographs will be the best way to preserve your arguments that the premises were properly maintained and hence you are entitled to return of the entire security deposit. As with every piece of litigation, preserving evidence will be critical.

Chapter 16: Keep saving on attorneys fees. Small Claims Court allows you to handle a case without a lawyer.

Chapter 1925 of the Ohio Revised Code addresses small claims court. Section 1925.01 mandates that every municipal and county court establish a small claims division to aid litigants in smaller disputes. Section 1925.02 provides that, with some exceptions, these small claims courts have jurisdiction to consider disputes less than $3,000.00. Generally speaking, small claims courts are used to resolve contract or negligence cases, but some disputes are expressly removed from the court's jurisdiction. For example, the small claims division cannot consider disputes regarding libel, slander, return of property, malicious prosecution, or matters which demand punitive damages. Nonetheless, the small claims court is well situated to handle most disputes less than $3,000.00.

Unless the plaintiff intends to present a claim on behalf of a corporation, a party may appear without an attorney and argue to the court. Generally speaking, a corporation will need to be represented by an attorney. Because corporations are distinct legal entities, some courts have concluded that the Ohio Revised Code requires that a corporation be represented by an attorney; otherwise, the person representing the corporation might be found to have engaged in the unauthorized practice of law. This is so even where there is only one shareholder. The Ohio Supreme Court has since concluded that a representative of the corporation may appear to present the claims so long as the individual does not engage in cross-examination or other acts of advocacy and so long as his actions are limited to appearing and completing preprinted court forms.[79] For those persons representing their own claims though, the small claims division may be the ideal venue.

The small claims court is also appealing because the clerks within the office of the clerk of courts are generally very friendly and helpful.

---

[79] *Cleveland Bar Assn. v. Pearlman* (2005), 106 Ohio St.3d 136.

Knowing that most people who present small claims are apprehensive and cost sensitive, they often make an extra effort to answer many basic procedural questions. And, with a filing fee in the $40.00-60.00 range, costs to the plaintiff are at a practical minimum.

That said, small claims litigation is litigation like any other. **[Tip]** Both the rules of civil procedure and rules of evidence themselves exempt small claims cases. Rule 1(C)(4) exempts small claims cases from the rules of civil procedure. As the proceedings are designed to move quickly, many of the mechanisms outlined in the rules of procedure would be impossible to implement in such short time frames.

> Small claims court works because the rules of procedure and evidence don't apply.

In a similar manner, the rules of evidence specifically exclude the rules from applying to small claims cases. Rule 101(C)(8) provides that the Ohio Rules of Evidence do not apply to "[p]roceedings in the small claims division of a county or municipal court." The following best describes the evidence that will be permitted in a small claims case: Referees obviously require some reliable evidence to prove a claim, but a referee, exercising some discretion, should not deny a layman justice through a formalistic application of the law of evidence. A small claims division is intended as a layman's forum. [80]

Hence, the small claims division is an ideal venue for persons to represent themselves in disputes with a value less than $3,000.00. As the forum is designed for laypersons to pursue their own claims, it is the most appropriate place to litigate without the assistance of an attorney. As attorney fees are often the practical barrier to pursuing claims, small claims courts are the only method of offering a realistic opportunity for parties to resolve disputes which although important to the litigants, involve claims of lesser monetary disputes.

---

[80] *Hines v. Somerville* (Oct. 19, 1995), Cuyahoga App. No. 68040, unreported.

That said, one must not confuse the small claims division of the municipal or county court with the general division of these courts. County courts are typically more rare. Sometimes difficult to comprehend, they are courts that cover the territory not covered by a municipal court within the county's territorial limits. In simplest terms, the jurisdiction of all courts are divided as monetary jurisdiction and subject matter jurisdiction. Section 1901.17 of the Ohio Revised Code provides that a municipal court has monetary jurisdiction over claims not exceeding $15,000.00. Section 1901.18 provides that the municipal court will have subject matter jurisdiction over disputes for the recovery of property, contract disputes, the foreclosure of liens on personal property, replevin, and eviction. As to county courts, Section 1907.03 also provides a $15,000.00 monetary jurisdiction. Section 1907.031 provides that, for the most part, the subject matter jurisdiction of the county court is the same as that of the municipal court.

It is critical again to understand that the county courts and the general division of the municipal courts are very different than small claims. The rules of evidence and civil procedure absolutely apply in these courts. Not understanding these rules can have dramatic effects on even the best lawsuits. As such, if one can't afford an attorney to handle such cases, it will be important to dedicate effort to best understand the procedures and to carefully review all documentation transmitted during the course of the litigation. Although no basic guide can provide enough to prepare someone to litigate a case, a basic reminder of the framework of a civil case might also provide some comfort.

Chapter 17: Sure, lawsuits are complicated, but they don't have to be a mystery.

Again, the simple reality is that an attorney will be better skilled to handle your case than will be you. That said, there are often reasons, typically financial, that hiring an attorney may not be practical - or simply impossible - for your family. Nonetheless, if a case is pending with you as either plaintiff or defendant, you are still going to need to do your best to address the matter so as to protect your family.

Although no simple guide to Ohio law can give you a complete explanation of the litigation process, the rules of evidence, the rules of procedure and all other issues associated with litigation, understanding a few basics may provide you some comfort. Often the mystery of the process alone can cause one to ignore the matter altogether. There simply can be no worse response. Having a little comfort with the process may eliminate some of this anxiety, thereby allowing you to think through the problem more clearly.

Understand first that the civil litigation system is designed to require and allow parties to state claims, to notice the adverse party, and to allow the adverse party to state their answer to the claims. There are only a few instances in the civil system where notice and an opportunity to respond will not be available. For the most part, understand that every pleading filed against you, requires notice to you from the opposing party and allows you an opportunity to respond. (If you are filing pleadings, you have a similar responsibility to send copies to the opposing party so that they may take advantage of their opportunity to respond.)

> You must provide the opposing party copies of everything you file with the court.

[Tip] The process is easily illustrated with the initiation of the lawsuit itself. Every lawsuit will start with the filing of a document known as a complaint.

131

Ohio is what is described as a "notice pleading state." In general terms, this document need only be clear enough to provide the opposing party an adequate notice of the claims against it. A complaint and a summons will be served on the defendants by the Clerk of Courts. Typically, all other documents filed with

> Lawsuits are complicated, but just remember the system requires notice and an opportunity to respond. Make sure you do.

the court must be served on the opposing party by the party filing the document; do not expect that the Clerk of Courts will serve these other documents for you.

With the filing of the complaint, the system allows the opposing party a period of time to respond in writing to the allegations. From the simplest perspective, Rules 8 and 12 of the Ohio Rules of Civil Procedure define the requirements for filing a complaint and an answer. Rule

> You will lose the case if you don't respond to the complaint.

12(A)(1) requires that the defendants respond to the

complaint by filing a written answer within 28 days. **[Trap]** You must respond to a complaint, otherwise Rule 55 will allow a plaintiff to request default judgment against you.

Along with an answer, a defendant is obligated to file any claims it might have against the plaintiff arising out of the same transaction. These claims are called counterclaims and are simply a complaint stated in response along with an answer. The plaintiff then, who would be the opposing party to the counterclaim, is obligated to respond to the counterclaim in a similar sort of answer.

Once these pleadings are closed, civil litigation moves to a process called "discovery." It is best to view discovery as the process by which parties exchange information to prepare their cases, to "discover" information; hence the name "discovery." The rules for discovery are found in Rules 26 through 37 of the Ohio Rules of Civil Procedure. There are a number of discovery tools permitted by the rules. The more typical are interrogatories, request for admissions, request for the production of documents and depositions.

There are certain formal ways that discovery is requested. If you were representing yourself and could only do one thing to acquire information for your case, send the opposing party a letter requesting specific information. Your letter should indicate that you request documents that you can identify by name; then request in general terms documents related to the subject of the litigation; request all expert reports; and then a "catch-all" request for any and all documents the opposing party intends to use at trial or to submit to any expert witnesses. [Although legal forms are never a substitute for the advice of counsel. You will find useful the *pro forma* discovery letter included in the appendix of forms.] You must also be sure to respond to the various discovery requests of the opposing party. If you don't, the court has certain discretion to sanction you by disallowing your evidence.

> Make sure you request in writing all documents and evidence from the opposing party.

If you could only know one other rule in the civil discovery process, it would be the consequences of the failure to answer a request for admission. Rule 36 of the Ohio Rules of Civil Procedure allows a party to propound what are referred to as requests for admission. These are simple statements which request that you admit or deny certain things. Often they are drafted to acquire admissions to essential issues in dispute to which an admission would be devastating to the opposing party. It is absolutely critical to understand that subsection (A) of Rule 36 specifically provides that "[t]he matter is admitted unless, within a period designated in the request, not less than twenty-eight days after service thereof or within such shorter or longer time as the court may allow, the party to whom the request is directed serves upon the party requesting the admission a written answer or

> DON'T FORGET - answer the admission.

> You must answer a request for admission or you effectively admit the question.

objection addressed to the matter, signed by the party or by his attorney." **[Trap]** In plain language, this means unless you deny the requested admission in writing within 28 days of receiving it, the law will presume you admitted the question. Cases are easily won and lost because of failures to answer request for admissions.

The next major procedure will be dispositive motions. "Dispositive motions" are motions designed to dispose of all or part of the case, hence the name "dispositive." The most typical dispositive motion, is a motion for summary judgment as provided by Rule 56 of the Ohio Rules of Civil Procedure. A motion for summary judgment is rather self-explanatory. It is a motion to grant judgment for one party in a summary fashion, without a trial, hence the name "summary judgment."

The procedure is rather simple, but does require an understanding of the rule. It allows the parties to submit very specific types of evidence to support arguments why judgment should be awarded for or against a party on all or some of the issues in the litigation. It is important to understand that Rule 56 only allows the court to consider certain evidence. The reason for this is obvious; if the court is going to eliminate a party's right to a trial, it must be based on reliable evidence. As such, Rule 56 only allows a motion for summary judgment to be based on "pleading, depositions, answers to interrogatories, written admissions affidavits, transcripts of evidence in the pending case, and written stipulations of evidence." Typically, motions for summary judgment are supported by the interrogatory responses and admissions of the opposing party, testimony from depositions, and affidavits of witnesses favorable to the party. **[Trap.]** A simple letter from a witness attached to the motion is not permissible; however, that same letter sworn before a notary with a notary seal may be permissible evidence.

The list of Rule 56 evidence also emphasizes the point that it is critical to request discovery as early in the litigation as possible. Again, ideally one would be represented by an attorney and take full advantage of the discovery process, but if that is not an option it is critical that the documents be requested from the opposing party early in the litigation.

Once dispositive motions are addressed and either awarded or rejected, in whole or in part, the remainder of the litigation will be scheduled for a trial. Mind you, a trial will be a very different thing altogether. If the matter is scheduled for a jury trial, the judge will likely provide little if any flexibility in either procedure or evidence. With a trial to the judge, the court may be a little more flexible with both, but understanding these procedures will be important.

Chapter 18: Can't lawyers learn to get along - why all the objections. What do you mean its hearsay...I heard it myself.

The procedure in a trial is rather formulaic for a number of reasons. In general terms, the procedure is as follows:

- Case can start with the jury selection;
- Followed by opening statements of both parties;
- Presentation of plaintiff's case with plaintiff's witnesses and cross-examination of the plaintiff's witnesses;
- Presentation of defendant's case, witnesses and cross-examination by plaintiff;
- Rebuttal case of plaintiff;
- Closing argument of the parties,
- Jury instructions and deliberation by the jury until verdict or mistrial.

Again, no basic guide can fully prepare one to handle a trial. But there are a few issues that typically arise during a trial which can cause those representing themselves much aggravation. If you could only understand two basic evidence concepts, know hearsay and foundation.

The hearsay concept can be rather aggravating even to trial lawyers. It has its origins in the phrase "by hear say."[81] Hearsay evidence is that evidence which was not observed by the witness testifying, but instead was relayed to the witness by another. That said, if you understand the technical definition of "hearsay evidence," you may understand that not everything told my another is inadmissible as hearsay. Rule 801(C) of the Ohio Rules of Evidence defines "hearsay" as "a statement, other than one made by the declarant while testifying at the trial or hearing, offered in evidence to prove the truth of the matter

> Subpoena the witness who actually saw or heard the event because hearsay is almost always not admitted. You can sometimes get a subpoena from the Clerk of Courts.

---

[81] http://dictionary.reference.com/browse/hearsay, July 25, 2009.

asserted." In as plain English as possible, "hearsay" is an out of court statement offered to prove what is asserted in that statement. That said, if the out of court statement is offered to prove something else, it is not by definition hearsay.

[Tip] A very simple example might serve to illustrate the analysis. Testimony that an out of court person told me the car was blue is hearsay if it is offered to prove the car was blue. If, for instance, the out of court witnesses statement that the car was blue was offered to prove the witnesses had seen the car, it may not be hearsay as it is offered to prove something other than the fact that the car was blue.

There are also a great number of exceptions to the rule that prohibits hearsay. It would be impossible to offer any useful explanation of all the exceptions in this basic guide. That said, an understanding of two concepts and two hearsay exceptions may help you handle your own case. Section 801(D)(2) of the Ohio

Rules of Evidence provides that an out of court statement offered to prove the truth of the matter asserted is not hearsay if it was the statement of a "party opponent," namely the plaintiff if you're the defendant and vice versa. In simplest terms, any witness may testify to hearing any statement of an opposing party. [82] This is not actually an exception to the hearsay prohibition; the rules exclude these prior statements of an opposing from the definition of hearsay.

> Statements by the opponent are never hearsay and always admissible if relevant.

Somewhat similar is the rule that allows prior out of court statements where the out of court statement is inconsistent with a witness's in court testimony. This is technically not a hearsay exception, but instead a rule that allows the prior statement to be offered to impeach the witness. In simple terms, if the out of court statement was

---

[82] Mind you, every piece of evidence, including statements of a party opponent must be relevant to the matter to be admissible.

different than the in court testimony, it is admissible to attack the witness's credibility. The prior statement is only admissible to prove the matter asserted, in other words as "substantive evidence," if it was given under oath and subject to cross-examination.

Again, it would be impossible to address them all, but there are two actual exceptions to the hearsay prohibition that arise rather often. They are the "excited utterance" and the "business records" exceptions. **[Tip]** All the hearsay exceptions are premised on the thought that although the out of court witness is not actually testifying in court, the out of court statements are otherwise reliable for some reason. With the "excited utterance" exception, the rules allow an out of court statement to come in to evidence to prove the assertion in the statement when the witness was "under the stress of excitement caused by the event or condition." Merely being upset will not be enough, the witness has to have been so excited that the clarity of observation and recollection were enhanced so to speak.

A typical example would be the statement of an out of court witness to a physical assault or traffic violation that may have caused an accident. The questioning of the in court witness will need to establish all the elements of the excited utterance prior to asking about the out of court statement. **[Tip]** With an assault case, a typical outline of the in court questioning would include:

1. Ms. Witness, where were you standing at the moment of the fight?
2. Were there any others nearby?
3. Did there appear to be anything obstructing the views of these other witnesses?
4. Did you hear anyone describe how the fight started?
5. Where and how far away was this person, was his view obstructed, etc.?
6. Before we talk about what he said, I want to talk about this person's demeanor?
7. Tell me about his condition?
8. Did you see his expressions? Tell me about his expressions?

9. Do you remember how he was talking, reacting, etc.?

10. Tell me what this witness said?

With these questions, the in court witness should be able to testify to what the out of court witness stated. For instance, if the out of court witness saw the that one person threw a devastating first punch, the out of court statement describing the punch would be admissible if the description was offered while still under the stress of witnessing the assault. If stated while still under the stress, the out of court description of the event should be admissible without the in court testimony of the person who witnessed the punch. A person who overheard the statement describing the punch would be permitted to testify instead. The key foundation for the evidence is outlining that the witnesses was reacting, talking, and gesturing as if he was under the stress of witnessing the assault. This should amount to an excited utterance and hence be admissible.

The other typical hearsay exception - and mind you again, there are so very many hearsay exceptions - is the "business records" exception. It is actually easiest to understand this "business records" exception if you remember it as "records of regularly conducted activity" which is the title used in the Ohio Rules of Evidence. The

> A credit card company will try to prove its case with the business records exception. Sometimes a debt purchaser may not be able to establish the elements for a business record so listen closely.

title alone helps one understand the foundation required to establish this hearsay exception. It is relevant when a party offers certain business records without the actual person who created the record. The law presumes that the records are accurate due to the routine and regular nature that the records are created.

For instance, where a business keeps a daily log of the calls service personnel are directed to or payments on credit card statements, the "business records" exception will allow the records into evidence without testimony of the actual author of the records. The questioning of the in court witness will need to establish first that the witness is familiar with the record keeping process. Second, the questioning will need to establish that the information in the report or record was recorded near the time it occurred and by a person with knowledge of the information recorded. [83] For example, a very basic foundation for business records for a service call would include:

1. What is your position with X Corp.
2. In that position, are you familiar with the record keeping process for service calls?
3. How is the log created, who is authorized to make entries in the log, how often is the log created, etc.?
4. Why is the record created?
5. Where is it kept?
6. (Procedurally, the witness will be handed the exhibit and asked to identify it.)
7. Is that the service log we've been discussing?

---

[83] The rule can also be used to prove that the absence of something in the record is evidence that it didn't occur.

8. Does that record include an entry for January 1, 2006?

9. Please tell the court what it indicates.

10. Most important, tell the court what it means.

These are two rather common exceptions to the hearsay prohibition. But they also serve to identify the important principles that will typically surround every hearsay exception, namely that the out of court testimony is for some reason otherwise reliable such that we don't need the out of court witness to testify. Understanding this concept may also help you in the heat of trial in dealing with objections to other testimony.

These exceptions also serve to demonstrate the importance of evidentiary foundation. The lack of an appropriate foundation is often another objection to the admission of testimony or evidence one will hear during trial. Foundation is critical at trial as every witness and piece of evidence requires an appropriate foundation before it can be considered by the trier of fact.

You will be best prepared if you understand

foundation in simple terms. Black's Law Dictionary defines "foundation" as "testimony which identifies the evidence sought to be admitted and connects it with the issue in question." [84] In clearer language, you must demonstrate that the testimony or evidence is what one says it is and that it is relevant to the matter at hand.

There can be very specific foundation requirements for certain types of evidence. **[Tip]** In many cases a sufficient foundation can be established by identifying your five "Ws." These are the same five "Ws" we were taught when doing our first elementary school book report:

> Foundation is who, what, when, where, why.

- **W**ho;
- **W**hat;
- **W**hen;

---

[84] Black's Law Dictionary 656 (6th Ed.) 1990.

- **W**here; and
- **W**hy.

The techniques used and psychology behind questioning witnesses can be very sophisticated. All the good and bad trial lawyers can describe for you their processes and include success stories to prove the validity of their respective theories. The five "Ws" is the simplest framework. Remember the law wants to know why a piece of evidence is relevant to the issue at hand and why it is reliable enough to be considered by a judge or jury. If you keep these two issues in mind, the concept of foundation becomes clearer. Use the five "Ws" to establish:

- Who the witness is in relation to the issue at hand;
- What the witness observed or heard;
- When the witness observed or heard;
- Where the witness was when he observed or heard; and
- Why the witness was where he was at when he observed or heard the incident.

Using the five "Ws" as a framework, you will

immediately identify for the court that the witness is important to the case; accordingly, his testimony should be carefully considered. You will then establish what specifically the witness observed about the case, and when and where the witness was when it was observed. The when and where "Ws" explain for the jury why the witness's observation is reliable as he was there at the time of and near the incident observed.

The "why" "W" is a little deeper. Explaining why the witness was there will help further explain why the witness' recollection is reliable. For instance, if the witness was there because it was his job to be there, his observation may have been clearer. Or, for instance, if the witnesses looked toward the incident because of a shocking sound, the recollection may be more permanent.

> When you hear an objection. Relax and try the five "Ws" first. That may correct the problem without you knowing why.

In short, there is no easy way to understand

the rules of evidence. An attorney should always be better skilled to handle trial matters. If having an attorney is not practical, you will be much better prepared to represent yourself if you keep these basic concepts in mind. Think back again to the issue of hearsay, understand why its disfavored and understand fundamentally why its exceptions are permitted. Underlying it all, remember the five "Ws" of story telling. Not only will they develop the story of your case, but they will help establish the necessary foundation for the various pieces of evidence you might present.

Chapter 19: Feel the power.

Hopefully, this short book is empowering. With a bit of patience and careful attention to the legal issues effecting your family, one can handle certain matters without the assistance of attorneys. In fact, lawyers have participated in the design of this system which also offers self-help opportunities for Ohio families. Most important, my profession has an honorable history of providing *pro bono* assistance to those in need. Every family should have a trusted lawyer - an advisor to turn to for all sort of legal and non-legal problems. Lawyers with broad practices encounter a wide array of problems effecting people on a daily basis. [Tip] Use your lawyer, not only as a legal advisor, but as a confidant and a guide to solving all sorts of problems. Candidly, solving problems unrelated to the law often provides a lawyer some of her greatest satisfaction.

APPENDIX OF FORMS

IN THE COURT OF COMMON PLEAS
_____COUNTY, OHIO

STATE OF OHIO	)	CASE NO: _____
Plaintiff,	)	JUDGE_____
-vs-	)	**MOTION FOR**
_____	)	**APPOINTMENT**
	)	**OF COUNSEL**
_____	)	
Defendant.	)	

Now comes the defendant, by and through counsel, and motions this Honorable Court, to appoint counsel for the defendant at State's expense. The undersigned testifies by way of this motion that he is indigent and cannot afford counsel.

WHEREFORE, the Defendant prays this Honorable Court for an Order appointing counsel for defense.

Respectfully submitted,

_____
Address
Telephone

CERTIFICATE OF SERVICE

    A true and accurate copy of the foregoing was served this ___ day of _____, 20_____ by ordinary U.S. Mail to the following:

Prosecutor _____
Address _____
_____

_____

IN THE COURT OF COMMON PLEAS
_____ COUNTY, OHIO

STATE OF OHIO	)	CASE NO:_____
Plaintiff,	)	JUDGE_____
-vs-	)	<u>ORDER</u>
_____	)	<u>APPOINTING</u>
	)	<u>COUNSEL</u>
_____	)	
Defendant.	)	

This matter came on for consideration upon the defendant's Motion for Appointment of Counsel. The Court finds the Defendant to be indigent, and therefore finds the motion to be well-taken. The Court appoints _____, Esq. as counsel for the defendant.

IT IS SO ORDERED.

_____
JUDGE

IN THE COURT OF COMMON PLEAS
JUVENILE DIVISION
_____ COUNTY, OHIO

IN THE MATTER OF) CASE NO.
_____)
)
Alleged _____) JUDGE
)
) REQUEST FOR
) DISCOVERY

Pursuant to Rule 24 of the Rules of Juvenile Procedure, the Defendant-Juvenile, requests that the prosecuting attorney produce discovery for inspection and copying at the office of _____, at _____. In the alternative, copies of documents responsive to this request may be mailed to the undersigned.

The documents requested are set out in Exhibit "A" attached hereto and incorporated herein.

Respectfully submitted,

_____
Address_____
Telephone_____

CERTIFICATE OF SERVICE

A true and accurate copy of the foregoing was served this ____ day of _____, 20_____ by ordinary U.S. Mail to the following:

Prosecutor _____

Address _____

_____

                    _____

EXHIBIT "A"

1. The names and last know addresses of each witness to the occurrence that forms the basis of the charge or defense;

2. Copies of any written statements made by any party or witness;

3. Transcriptions, recordings, and summaries of any oral statements of any party or witness, except the work product of counsel;

4. Any scientific or other reprots that a party intends to introduce at the hearing or that pertain to physical evidence that a party intends to introduce;

5. Photographs and any physical evidence which a party intends to introduce at the hearing;

6. Other evidence favorable to the requesting party and relevant to the subject matter involved in the pending action.

7. Dispatch recordings and other such records.

Date: _____

Prosecutor _____
Address: _____
_____

Re: Case Name:_____
Case Number: _____

Request for Discovery, Demand for a Bill of Particulars, and for Notice of Intention to Use Evidence.

Dear Prosecutor:

I am making a demand for all of the information which I am entitled to pursuant to Criminal Rules 16, 7(E), and 12(D)(2), as well as any other Federal or State constitutional provision, Ohio Revised Code provision, or Rule of Criminal Procedure.

As such, the defendant hereby requests the following information:

1. Any and all statements made by the defendant, whether they be written, recorded, oral or summaries of any such statement;
2. Any recorded testimony of the defendant or co-defendant before a Grand Jury;
3. A complete copy of the defendant's prior criminal record, if any;

4. A complete written list of any books, papers, documents, photographs, tangible objects, buildings or places, or copies or portions thereof relevant to the above captioned matter;

5. Any reports of tests, or mental or physical examinations, or any specific tests or experiments relevant to the above captioned matter;

6. A written list of the names and addresses of all witnesses whom the prosecuting attorney intends to call at trial, together with any record or prior felony convictions of any such witnesses;

7. A list of all evidence known or which may become known to the prosecuting attorney, favorable to the defendant and material either to guilt or punishment;

8. A list of the evidence the prosecution intends to use in chief at trial of the above captioned matter.

10. A copy or an opportunity to review any and all dispatch records, logs or audio recording and video recordings.

Further, under *Brady vs. Maryland* (1963), 373 U.S. 82 and *United States vs. Agurs* (1977), 427 U.S. 97, it is my belief that *you are duty bound to disclose any unrequested evidence which creates a reasonable doubt of guilt and any doubt you may have concerning the materiality of evidence must be disclosed to the accused.*

If a response is not received within five (5) days from this date, we will consider it a refusal. Please contact my office with any questions.

Yours truly,

_____

LAST WILL & TESTAMENT OF

I, _____, of the City of _____, County of _____, and State of Ohio, being of lawful age and of sound and disposing mind and memory, do hereby publish and declare this to be my Last Will and Testament, and I hereby revoke any and all Wills and/or codicils heretofore made by me.

ITEM I

I direct that all of my just debts and funeral expenses be first paid out of my estate as soon after my decease as is practicable.

ITEM II

I hereby give, devise and bequeath all the rest, residue and remainder of my property, of whatever kind and nature, whether real, personal or mixed, and wheresoever the same may be situated at the time of my decease to my wife, _____, to be hers absolutely and in fee simple.

ITEM III

In the event my wife, _____, should predecease me or die within sixty (60) days of the date of my death or in the case my said wife, _____, and I should die of a common disaster or accident and/or under such circumstances that the precedence in death cannot be determined, then ITEM II, of this, my Last Will and Testament, shall have no effect, and in any one or more of said events, I give, devise and bequeath all the rest, residue and remainder of my property, of whatever kind and nature, and whether real, personal or mixed, and wheresoever the same may be situated, which I may own or have the right to dispose of at the time of my decease to my daughter _____and my stepson _____equally as set forth in Item IV hereafter.

ITEM IV

In the event that either my daughter, _____, or my stepson, _____, are not yet twenty-five (25) years of age or has not yet completed course work for an undergraduate college degree, which ever shall occur first, at the time of my death, and in the event that said child or stepchild are to receive, as beneficiary, a share of the proceeds from my estate as provided in Item III above, then said child's or stepchild's share or shares I give, devise and bequeath to _____ as Trustee for the benefit of said child or stepchild, subject to the following terms and conditions:

>(a) The Trustee shall hold, manage, invest and reinvest the trust property, shall collect the income therefrom, and is authorized and empowered to pay to said child or stepchild, or to expend for his/her benefit, so much of the principal and current or accumulated interest therefrom, and in such amounts and manner as the Trustee may deem necessary or proper, to provide for his/her suitable maintenance, support, health, welfare and education (including college and professional education, if appropriate), after taking into consideration his/her income and means of support from other sources. Any amounts of income which the Trustee shall determine not to distribute or to expend for the benefit of said child or stepchild shall be accumulated.

(b) Upon both my child and stepchild attaining the age of twenty-five (25) years old or having completed course work for an undergraduate college degree, which ever shall occur first, the Trustee shall distribute said child's or stepchild's share, as it shall then exist, both principal and income, to the child or stepchild free and discharged of all trusts.

(c) In the event of the death of either my child or stepchild before receiving distribution in full of the share of the trust property held for his/her benefit, the share of the trust property so held or intended to be held for the benefit of such deceased child or stepchild's shall vest in and be distributed to his/her living issue, per stirpes; but if any of such issues has not yet attained the age of twenty-five (25) years of age, the Trustee is authorized and empowered to pay to such one or to expend for such issue's benefit, so much of the principal and current or accumulated income as the Trustee may deem necessary or proper to provide for such issue's suitable maintenance, support, health, welfare and education (including college and professional education). Any amounts of income which the Trustee shall determine not to distribute or to expend for the benefit of such one shall be accumulated.

(d) If a child or stepchild for whose benefit the Trustee holds a share of the trust property dies before receiving distribution in full, without issue surviving him/her, then the share of the trust property for such deceased child or stepchild shall vest in and be distributed to my then living remaining child or stepchild, provided, however, that any such amount shall be added to said living child's or stepchild's trust property if said living child or stepchild is under the age of twenty-five (25) years old or has not yet completed course work for an undergraduate college degree, which ever shall occur first, at the time of receipt of property pursuant to this paragraph. The Trustee shall then manage said additional trust property as if originally constituting a part of said living child's trust property.

(e) In the event that _____ can not serve as Trustee or continue to serve as

Trustee for _____ and _____, then I request the appointment of_____ as alternate Trustee, granting to her all powers and duties as set forth above for _____.

ITEM V

I hereby nominate and appoint my wife, _____, the Executrix of this, my Last Will and Testament, authorizing and empowering my said Executrix to compound, compromise, settle and adjust all debts and claims which may be presented to or be due to my estate and to sell at public or private sale at such prices and upon such terms of credit or private sale, as he may deem advisable, the whole or any part of my real or personal property and to execute deeds and other proper instruments of conveyance thereof to the purchaser or purchasers.

ITEM VI

I direct that no bond be required of any fiduciary named in this will.

ITEM VII

In the event _____, refuses or is for any reason unable to act as Executor, I nominate and appoint_____ as Executor and give to him the same powers as given to _____.

IN WITNESS WHEREOF, I have hereunto set my hand and published and declared this to be my Last Will and Testament at City of _____, Ohio, this _____ day of _____, 20_____.

_____

Print: _____

Signed and acknowledged by _____ as his Last Will and Testament in our presence and by us subscribed to as attesting witnesses in his presence and at his request and in the presence of each other, _____, in our opinion, of sound and disposing mind and memory, and under no restraint or undue influence whatsoever at city of _____, Ohio, this ____ day of _____, 20_____.

Witnessed by:

_____ at _____
_____   _____

_____ at _____
_____   _____

STATE OF OHIO)
) SS:
COUNTY OF _____)

BEFORE ME, a Notary Public in and for said State and County; personally appeared _____ who acknowledged that (s)he did execute the foregoing and that it is (her) his free act and deed.

IN WITNESS WHEREOF, I have hereunto set my hand and official seal this ____ day of _____, 20____.

_____
NOTARY PUBLIC

Durable General Power of Attorney

I, _____, City of _____, County of _____, State of Ohio, hereby appoints _____, my lawful attorney-in-fact, to act for me and in my name for all contracts, deeds, leases, assignments, obligations, writings, assurances, releases and other instruments which to said attorney may seem proper in connection with any matter in which I may be interested, and generally to act for me and in my name in all matters affecting my business or property, real or personal, with the same effect as though I were personally present and acting for myself; also granting full power to substitute one or more persons in the place of said attorney and to revoke any such substitution; and hereby ratifying and confirming whatever said attorney or substitute may do under this Power of Attorney.

Without limiting said general powers, I hereby specifically authorize said attorney or substitute to do the following for me and in my name: to enter upon or into and to take possession of any of my property, real or personal, including any safe deposit box standing in my name and its contents, and to demand, receive and receipt for any and all sums of money or property, real or personal, now or hereafter due to me, including any bank or savings and loan association deposit in my name; to deposit in any bank or savings and loan association any and all bills, accounts, mortgages, indebtedness, taxes, assessments, claims and demands now or hereafter payable by me; to sign, endorse and deliver all checks, drafts and instruments of like nature payable to me or by me as to aid attorney may seem proper; to borrow money and to sign and deliver any bond, note or other evidence of debt or other instrument in writing necessary or proper in connection with said loan, and to endorse, assign, pledge, mortgage and hypothecate any and all of my property, real or personal, as security for such loan, on such terms as to said attorney may seem proper; to sell, lease and dispose of any or all of my property, real or personal, for such prices and upon such terms of credit or otherwise as to said attorney may seem proper, and to execute and deliver to the purchasers or lessees of such property appropriate contracts, bills of sale, leases, assignments, deeds, land contract and other instruments of conveyance or transfer thereof, with or without covenants of warranty or similar covenants; to vote any shares of stock in any corporation standing in my name, with the full power of substitution in the exercise of such rights, and for said purpose to execute and deliver all necessary proxies; to insure any of my property, real or personal, in such amounts and on such terms as to said attorney may seem proper; to buy or otherwise acquire and hold, in such name or names as to said attorney may seem proper, property, real or personal, for such prices and upon such terms of credit or otherwise as to said attorney shall see proper, and to sign and deliver such instruments and make such payments as may be appropriate or incidental to any such purchase, acquisition or holding; to commence and carry on, or to defend, at law or in equity, all actions, suits and other proceedings in which I or my real or personal property may be in any way concerned; to compound, compromise, settle and adjust all claims (including tax claims) in favor of or against me, upon such terms as to said attorney may seem proper; to prepare, execute and file any tax returns, local state or federal, and any refund claims thereon; to assign and convey any or all of my property, real or personal, to any trust established by me or by others over which I have unrestricted rights of revocation or withdrawal, at such times as said attorney deems appropriate, and to execute and deliver to the trustee appropriate assignments, deeds and other instruments of conveyance or transfer thereof, even if said attorney is trustee of such trust; and to employ and pay reasonable compensation to agents, accounts, attorneys and investment counsel to assist in the exercise of any of the foregoing powers.

     This Power of Attorney shall only be effective during a time in which I am either incompetent or incapable of handling my own affairs. This Power of Attorney may be terminated either by me or by said attorney by giving written notice of such termination to the other. An executed duplicate of this Power of Attorney, or a photostatic copy thereof, delivered by me or by said attorney to any third party will be conclusive against me and said attorney as to such third party that this Power of Attorney has not been terminated and will continue in effect until such third party is advised by written notice from me or from said attorney of such termination. This Power of Attorney shall be governed by Ohio law.

I hereby reserve all rights on my part to do personally any act which said attorney is hereby authorized to perform, and to grant similar powers of attorney to others.

I give to _____, through this Power of Attorney, the absolute right to make gifts.

I have signed this Power of Attorney this ___ day of _____, 20_____

_____

Print: _____

Signed and acknowledged in the presence of:

Witnessed by:

_____   at _____

_____   _____

_____   at _____

_____   _____

STATE OF OHIO   )
) SS
COUNTY OF _____   )

    Personally appeared before me, a Notary Public for said county and state, _____, who acknowledged that she did sign this Power of Attorney, and that it is her free act and deed.

    I have signed and sealed this Power of Attorney at city of _____, Ohio, this ____ day of _____, 20____.

_____
NOTARY PUBLIC

Date _____

Attorney _____
Address _____

_____

Re: Case name_____
     Case number. _____

Dear Attorney:

Accept this informal letter as a request for discovery. You are hereby requested to answer under oath, the Interrogatories below, and produce each document requested and serve the responses to my address at _____Street, City of _____, Ohio, within twenty-eight (28) days of the time service is made upon you through your attorney and in accordance with Ohio Civil Rule of Procedure 33, 34, and 36.

<u>INTERROGATORY NO. 1</u> : State with specificity exactly what I did to create the liability as expressed in the complaint in this matter.

<u>ANSWER</u>:

INTERROGATORY NO. 2 : Identify the name, address, telephone number, and occupation of any and all persons with knowledge of the facts or occurrences which are the basis of the allegations in the complaint.

ANSWER:

INTERROGATORY NO. 3: Identify the name, address, telephone number, and occupation of any and all persons you expect to call to testify in this matter and the substance of their testimony.

ANSWER:

INTERROGATORY NO. 4: Identify the name, address, telephone number, and occupation of any and all experts you expect to call to testify in this matter, their qualifications, and the substance of their testimony.

ANSWER:

REQUEST FOR PRODUCTION OF DOCUMENTS NO. 1: Provide any and all documents, letters, reports, photographs, recordings or other such documents you intend to produce at trial or arbitration of this matter and any such document which supports the claims for relief stated in the complaint.

REQUEST FOR PRODUCTION OF DOCUMENTS NO. 2: Provide any and all expert reports and/or statements, along with documents reviewed, generated, or provided in support thereof.

REQUEST FOR PRODUCTION OF DOCUMENTS NO. 3: Provide copies of all photographs taken by you, by your representative or at your direction of the incident or of the damages sustained as a result of the incident.

REQUEST FOR PRODUCTION OF DOCUMENTS NO. 4: Provide copies of all communication, including but not limited to, correspondence and email, between plaintiff or its representatives and defendant.

Should you have any questions, contact me directly.

Truly yours,

_____

INDEX

abused child	50-52
abused, neglected, or dependent children	50-52
Adam Walsh Act	44-45
admissions	132-136
answer	132
appointed counsel	54-57
asset distribution	58
automobile searches	36
bank garnishment	93-98
bug infestation	115-116
business records	145-148
complaint	131
constructive eviction	115
consumer protection laws	84-90
Consumer Sales Practices Act	89-90
counterclaims	119, 133
credit card contract	80
credit card debt	76-92
deed in lieu of foreclosure	110-111
default judgment	133

delinquent child	42-45
Department of Youth Services (DYS)	43-45
dependent child	52-53
depositions	133-134
detention incarceration	43-45
discovery	133-134
dispositions	42-45
dispositive motions	136-137
education neglect	51
emergency guardianship	73
estate tax	68-70
eviction	118-120
evidentiary foundation	148-152
exceptions to the warrant requirement	34-36
excited utterance	143-145
exclusionary rule	37
Federal Adam Walsh Act	44-45
Federal Fair Debt Collection Practice Act	84-90
forbearance agreement	106-107
forcible entry and detainer	118
foreclosure	101

foundation	148-152
Fourth Amendment	34-37
frisk	36-37
garnishing bank accounts	97-98
garnishment of earnings	97-98
garnishment of other than earnings	97-98
garnishment of wages	93-96
Gideon v. Wainwright	54-57
guardian	71-75
guardianships	71-75
health care power of attorney	63-67
hearsay	141
hearsay exception	141-148
incompetent	71-72
indigent	54-57
interim guardianship	73
interrogatories	133-134
juvenile delinquent sex offenders	20
Juvenile Justice Reform Act	17-22
landlord obligations	113-117
landlord's duty to make repairs	117-118

least restrictive alternative 73

limited guardianship 73

living will 63-67

Mapp v. Ohio 38-39

Megan's Law 20

Miranda 25-33

Miranda v. Arizona 27

Miranda Warnings 25-33

mortgage obligations 100

motion for relief from judgment 96

motion for summary judgment 136-138

neglected child 51-52

negligent entrustment 48-49

New Jersey v. T.L.O 38

parental liability 46-49

party opponent 142-143

prior statement 142-143

production of documents 133-134

pupil's locker 38

R.C. 2111.01(A) and (B) 71-73

R.C. 2111.13 73-74

R.C. 2111.151 73-74
R.C. 2151.01 19
R.C. 2151.03 51-52
R.C. 2151.04 51-52
R.C. 2151.353 53
R.C. 2329.66(A)(13) 95-97
R.C. 5321.05 116-117
R.C. 5321.07 117-119
R.C. 5321.16 121-122
refinancing 105-106
right to appointed counsel 54-57
Rules of Evidence 126
school property 38-39
security deposits 121-123
sex offender registration 20, 44-45
short sale 106-108
Sixth Amendment 54-57
small claims court 124-129
taxation 68-70, 82-83, 109-110
tenant's ability to withhold rent 117-118
tenant's duty to maintain the premises 116

tenant obligations 116
tenant remedies 117-118
Terry v. Ohio 36-37
trial 139
Unified Credit 69
waiver of Miranda Rights 32-33
ward 71-75
warrant 36
will 58-63
withholding rent 117-118

JUST A SAMPLING OF
HOW TO USE THIS BOOK

* Out with friends, your minor son vandalized some property.

    TURN TO CHAPTERS 1, 2, 3, 4, 5 AND 7.

* Your parents can no longer manage their affairs.

    TURN TO CHAPTER 10.

* You fell behind on your credit cards and mortgage.

    TURN TO CHAPTERS 11, 12, AND 13.

* You are in a landlord-tenant dispute.

    TURN TO CHAPTERS 14, 15, 17, AND 18.

* Someone is trying to garnish your wages.

    TURN TO CHAPTER 12.

* You got sued or need to sue.

    TURN TO CHAPTERS 16, 17 AND 18.

ABOUT THE AUTHOR

Joseph R. "Randy" Klammer is the son of a lawyer and practices with his wife, Darya Klammer. They have two children. He was elected President of the Lake County Bar Association. In 2008, he was a speaker at the Superstars Seminar of the Ohio Association of Criminal Defense Attorneys. He has a number of articles to his name. This is his first book.

Both he and Darya are former assistant county prosecutors having handled criminal matters ranging from juvenile delinquency to adult murder. A significant portion of his practice is dedicated to criminal defense.

As the Law Director to a local city, he routinely evaluates zoning and building regulations. A considerable portion of his practice is dedicated to the constitutionality of zoning classifications, construction disputes, and land use rights.

He is increasingly proud that his practice has a general aspect to it which allows clients to call on him for all sort of legal matters. He, of course, would welcome the opportunity to meet with any reader should the advice of a lawyer be necessary.

Contact him directly at:
www.KLAMMERLAW.com

Made in the USA
Charleston, SC
25 October 2013